Anonymous

Comes out of the Shadows
To Brief the Whitehouse About UFOs

Transcript by Linda Moulton Howe (1998)
Compilation and Editing by
C. Ronald Garner at the Principal's Request
2010-2015

Alien Encounters Press
PO Box 1522 Stockbridge, MA 01262
www.alienencounterspress.com

Ordering Information:
Quantity sales. Special discounts are available on quantity purchases by corporations, associations, and others. For details, contact the "Special Sales Department" at the address above.

Anonymous: A CIA Adminstrator/Army Crytographer Comes Out of the Shadows to brief the Whitehouse on UFOs
ISBN 978-1-936517-84-8

Dedication

To Anonymous for his Courage and Dedication to his Country. And to all those "Anonymous" whose lost their lives to serve Government Secrecy. Your dedication and Sacrifices will never be forgotten.

Post Script Dedication: The writer/editor herein, C. Ronald Garner, confirms his commitment upon the publication of this book to the person whose narrative is outlined on these pages and to to his family not to reveal whether the person is dead or alive and never to reveal his true identity until such time that the family agrees to such disclosure. We are all subject to the Manifest Destiny of Celestial Influence.

"I Can Assure You The Flying Saucers, Given That They Exist, Are Not Constructed By Any Power On Earth."
-Former U.S. President Harry S. Truman - Press conference, Washington DC, April 4, 1950.

I Would Do It [Aid The Army Air Force In Its Investigations] But Before Agreeing To It We Must Insist Upon Full Access To The Discs Recovered. For Instance In The La* Case The Army Grabbed It And Would Not Let Us Have It For Cursory Examination." --From A *Handwritten Notation At The Bottom Of A Now Declassified Memo. (Asterisk Added, See Below) Quote About Secret Government Without Checks And Balances. "*
J. Edgar Hoover, Director of the FBI

"*I feel that the Air Force has not been giving out all the available information on the Unidentified Flying Objects. You cannot disregard so many unimpeachable sources.*"
-John W. McCormack, Former Speaker of the House, January 1965

"*I Occasionally Think How Quickly Our Differences, Worldwide, Would Vanish If We Were Facing An Alien Threat From Outside This World.*"
-Former U.S. President Ronald Reagan, In A Speech With President Mikhail Gorbachev, in 1988

C. Ronald Garner Bio

C. Ronald Garner is one of the most well respected UFO/Paranormal Researcher in the United States today. He is regarded for the thorough and journalistic approach to his research which has led to the inner sanctum of those ready to share above top secret information. Garner, a researcher for over 30 years has remained purposefully unacknowledged for many of the ground-breaking contributions he has made to the credible UFO literature. He is the uncredited Executive Producer of the "Citizen Hearings on UFO Disclosure" (National Press Club April/ May 2013)

C. Ronald Garner is a documentary Filmmaker with many of his films now available on DVD through his website. He is the former Co-owner of the Roswell UFO Enigma Museum (currently in storage Roswell N.M.) - Official videographer for The Society for Scientific Exploration – Princeton N.J. and has produced three different Radio Shows in Los Angeles focusing on topics of UFOs and the Paranormal. A veteran of television Garner was a Line Producer for the TV Program -- "The Other Side" -He has also been Public Relations Director for APRT Association for Past Life Research & Therapy - Organizer for various UFO Conferences & Events

Garner has been a guest on Coast to Coast Radio and his work has been used as research for such shows as "Ancient Aliens" on the History Channel. Follow his blog on www.alienencounterspress.com and visit his personal website at www.area51thetruth.com.

Preface

By C. Ronald Garner

When I was a teenager a neighbor gave me a book "Flying Saucers Have Landed" by George Adamski. I have been hooked on the subject ever since. My serious investigations began in 1982 while I was working for a mortgage company in Beverly Hills California. The woman manager told me that her brother worked at Area 51 and had met a rather strange person who also worked there. I was hoping that by strange she meant extraterrestrial so I tried to interview her brother. I got nowhere because he was reluctant to speak to me. He said there was a white van with a dish antenna that frequented his neighborhood. His suspicion was he was the target of its surveillance. Though I was intrigued, I let it drop.

In 1989 I was in Las Vegas when CBS TV conducted interviews between reporter George Knapp and physicist Bob Lazar. These interviews are famous among UFO enthusiasts because of their revelations. So seven years had passed and here was another Area 51 employee, basically, telling a very similar story. Bob's corroborative narrative really got my attention. I decided in the early 1990s that all of the reports of lights in the sky were never going to tell the real story behind the phenomena. I wanted to find out about the pilots inside those "Lights."

In 1993-94 I attended lectures by an avionics engineer whose name was Bill Uhouse. His story was riveting because he told of actually working with live ET people at Los Alamos and at Area 51. The off worlders came here to help our engineers and scientists build craft and other hardware to boot strap our civilization to a better world. Later I met his son who confirmed his father's testimony in every detail.

Then in 1997 I became aware of the person who provided the information for this book. He was a cryptographer for the US Army and then was recruited into the CIA. The time frame was 1956-1960. I have code named him "Anonymous." I have verified his story from all members of his family as well as public records.

The reason I have waited until now to publish his account is because "Anonymous" and his family did not want his story to become public, initially, until after his death. But in December 2010 at a Christmas lunch his son and daughter gave me the go ahead to begin making the story public. This book is being released in time for an unprecedented effort to persuade our government to finally reveal the truth of ongoing encounters with extraterrestrials that have been happening for millennia. The secondary purpose is to end the Truth Embargo of all of the Black Operations projects run by a separate "government" referred to as Majestic 12. This powerful group is not governed by any checks and balances. Throughout history even many of our presidents were kept out of the information loop. There is much speculation about the reasons for this non-disclosure. Some top level researchers surmise that there is too much money and power involved in keeping technology and other secrets away from the American and world public. Imagine a world without the need for energy, where all energy resources were free? Perhaps this is what the off worlders had to offer us. Instead of allowing us to participate in a free government according to our constitution, we have been kept in the dark.

We Can Handle The Truth!

Anonymous, now referred to as anonymous, is near death. You can find videos of his interviews on my website: area51thetruth.com. He has revealed his face but not his name. When he finished the first set of interviews with investigative reporter Linda Moulton Howe he was greeted outside of a grocery store by a black sedan with "men in black." The interviews had been conducted in person so they must have had Anonymous and Linda under some kind of surveillance. They made it clear he was not to continue telling his story.
Anonymous kept his secret for over 50 years but in sharing this information he has said that a weight has been lifted off his shoulders. Many of those who were privy to these secrets took them to their graves. He believes we have a right to know the Truth and he will now be able to go to his final rest in peace.

Sincerely,
C. Ronald Garner
Producer-Stargate Productions

Introduction

Area 51 Whistle blowers
This Is a True Story! by C. Ronald Garner

This book represents an attempt at setting the record straight about what our government knew about the "UFO Problem" beginning in the late 1950's and continuing until the present. Here in the first decade of the 21st Century the unfortunate truth is that all of the intelligence agencies in general, but the C.I.A. in particular, are guilty of hubris, in the extreme, by not allowing the governing authorities, namely the United States Congress, and main stream scientists to know that we are being visited, we have the craft the bodies and the people from another star system. Maybe it was necessary during the cold war but that time is long past. We Are Not Alone In The Universe! The Church committee hearings back in the 1970's were only the proverbial tip of many Black Operations icebergs that were exposed. To this day, the agencies have continued to grow ever more contemptuous. - We Can Handle The Truth!

Consequently in this investigative reporter's opinion the Intelligence Agencies with their Black Operations have consciously and blatantly violated the United States of America's Constitution and placed themselves "Above The Law!"

The Most Important UFO/ET Story in History

In 1997 I was working for a publishing company in San Diego California. One of my fellow coworkers knew that my primary interest was in the UFO field. We went to lunch one day and he began to tell me the most amazing story about his father-in—law. I subsequently confirmed his story by talking to his wife the daughter of the principle in this narrative.

This is the story they told me about their father and later confirmed by Anonymous himself

For the purposes of this treatise I will call him by a code name "Anonymous" because he wishes to remain anonymous for now. Throughout his time in the CIA he used several alias names. He is now referred to as Anonymous as he has chosen to come forward to reveal his story. He has not, however, revealed his real name and it will not be made known until after his death. Anonymous served as a first lieutenant with the US Army signal corps and was a CIA administrator at an army base in the eastern United States from 1957 to 1960. I have seen the documentation.

Back in 1957 to 1960 period, Anonymous taught radio operations and cryptography to Army Signal Corps officers under a false identification assigned to him by the CIA, for which he also worked. The head of that Signal Corps School had worked for the OSS during World War II. The OSS was the Office of Strategic Services which became the Central Intelligence Agency in 1947. In addition to teaching, Anonymous's CIA boss at the Army base, asked Anonymous to help analyze Top Secret cases gathered for the Air Force's Project Blue book investigation of unidentified flying objects.

Even though the public and media were later told there was nothing to UFOs and the Air Force was not interested, Anonymous said the truth was that highly sensitive and unexplained Blue Book case files were gathered in Washington D.C. and sent to Fort Belvoir, Virginia, and then re-routed to different CIA field offices for further study. One of those CIA analyses was at the Army base in which Anonymous and his boss worked with cryptography and radio operations.

Anonymous with his CIA boss were sent to the Papoose Mountain range on the edge of Groom Lake, Area 51, Nellis AFB Nevada, in august 1958. There with his boss and three other CIA agents, Anonymous toured with the USAF Colonel identified only as "Jim" to see disk craft inside a small mountain and a living, telepathic "Extraterrestrial Biological Entity, dressed in human civilian clothing to be more psychologically acceptable, Anonymous thought.

Anonymous's children told me that their father's security oath expired 35 years after he got out of the Army and CIA in 1960. That period ended in 1995, so Anonymous told his children that he felt he was not doing anything wrong by discussing with them his extraordinary firsthand knowledge and experiences concerning "Extraterrestrials", the word used to describe them in Top Secret classified files Anonymous read and analyzed from CIA headquarters in Langley, Virginia.

"Official" Version

At the base he was assigned to study photographs, drawings and film of Unidentified Craft and Beings. He said he and his boss were part of one of the groups investigating the unexplained phenomena. He knew when they closed down the "Official" Project Blue book files that the whole story had not been revealed. The Air Force said they had found very little that wasn't explainable. That was actually true because anything they could not explain away as conventional phenomena would be sent to Ft. Belvoir in Virginia and distributed to other military units. In some cases the FBI was asked to investigate.

He told his children Bill and Ester (code names) that he and his supervisor went to Area 51 in August 1958. They were told he was attending a meeting of all CIA personnel from this country, overseas, and the Far East. They wanted the meeting held there so that the assets that were directly involved with the "Secret" Blue Book project could be briefed and see the evidence for themselves. He said there were only 5 members from his US Army base at the meeting inside the base at Area 51 S-4. In his testimony, he said the other CIA agents were not with his group that interviewed the ET. The Far East and Central American agents were not allowed in at that time. He didn't know if they went in later or not.

He said they got into a small mini bus and did not stop to go into any other buildings. It was about 10 miles from the landing strip at Area 51 proper. He went on to tell his daughter and son-in-law that they did take him to the storage unit for U-2s. and the SR-71 Blackbirds that the Air Force was flying at that time. They were there a short time and were then driven to another secret location about eight miles further down the dry lake bed.

Further, he reported the third and final area they visited was where they had stored highly classified material. Here they stopped and went into an office-type atmosphere where they were met by a colonel that took them on tour. He took them down a walkway into a hangar area that had been carved out of the mountain. (Papoose Mountain Range). There were six covert agents in the group. They passed through different areas where there were other workers, office personnel, and scientists working on various secret projects. Finally they arrived at the craft area and walked around the various types of disc craft. The reason they wanted them to see the actual craft was so that when they looked at pictures sent to them in Project Blue Book Secret files they would be able to tell the difference between hoaxed or mistaken aerial phenomena. He said he never worked under his real name. It was always a CIA assigned alias.

He said that as soon as they got into the hangar area they saw two small craft, kind of a dull silver color not real shiny or bright, about 20 feet in diameter. Some had a carved out back section of the craft (Note: Like the craft seen by Kenneth Arnold in June 1947 over Seattle) He said they were not allowed to go down and touch them. They were on this walk way above the craft. (Note: Like a catwalk as described by other people interviewed by Ron Gamer) Again, they were not allowed to touch any of the craft. (Note: Bob Lazar's testimony was that he was not only allowed to touch but was instructed to go inside the craft when he worked at Area 51 in 1989)

He said that there were 7 to 10 craft visible from his vantage point. One of the most important things in this interview was that some of the craft were of German Origin the Vril and Haunebu variety that the US had captured after World War II from secret bases in the German mountains somewhere around Peenemunde. (Note: Of Paper clip fame) He said they were all disk shaped but some had larger bottom areas that extended down the same distance as they extended up, and they were different colors. The larger ones in the rear were a real dark gray color. Some of the other types were lighter in color, but maybe like a light or medium brown type color. The larger ones in the rear had real large top units and large bottom units to them and were sitting on steel saw horses to hold them above the surface of the floor. .

He described the propulsion system as anti-matter and anti-gravity. (Note: Same as noted by Bob Lazar's description) The group was trying to find out how it worked without any sign of a physical motor. The entire disc seemed to be similar to an electronic circuit which could make it fly. They knew it was similar to an electronic circuit because, he was told, that our pilots tried to fly them and said it was like a battery electrical unit and worked with ant-gravitational electromagnetic drive. The pilots further reported that the saucer itself was like a drive for the ship. Anonymous said the inside was coated with nickel and was similar to a giant electronic circuit. He went on to say the aliens were needed to engage or complete the circuit because they were tied in, having headbands that could act to control the craft. . He also said that they had finger control board panels to direct the flight character-istics.

(Note: See the Ray Santilli "Alien Autopsy" film clips)

He said he saw the circuit pallets. The scientists were trying to understand how the electronic circuitry worked as there was no evidence of wiring. Sometime later they found that when they had the "saucers" at Groom Lake, the scientists used microscopes to check over the fingertip control panels; they discovered small fibers going out from the panel. They concluded that there was a type of fiber optic electrical transmission throughout the craft. It was all done with light. The report that he read said that when they looked inside the craft, it was glowing with a real thin light from all the circuitry fiber optics on hoard. Reverse engineering of the alien technology produced our fiber optic technology of today. (Note: See the book The Day After Roswell by the late Col. Phil Corso Retired Army). The Colonel who was conducting the tour told the assembled Army group that some of these craft were picked up and captured in different parts of the world.

Visiting the Gray-Skinned Extra Terrestrial Biological Entity (code named: Eben)

Anonymous continues: "We went from the hangar area, where the saucers were, out to a covered walkway and into what I would call an office complex because it was a bunch of small rooms and offices. There they had a special room for viewing that had a one way window in it, one way mirror, rather, and we could look through the window into this small office where the Being was inside there. He was not able to see us through the window because there was a mirror on his side of the wall.

They told us that the Being spoke telepathically and the other four people went into the Being's room to try communicating. The Being was, I think, what the Colonel called a 'Gray'. He had the large head and bigger eyes, kind of slanted bigger eyes—he looked like he was wearing sunglasses because the lenses were real dark. A kind of a slim face down to a peaked chin with just a little nose area and a tiny slit of a mouth and just holes in the side of his head for ear openings. He or "it" was about five feet tall. It was grayish-looking through the window. It looked almost like a canvas or something that had graininess to it. Not real smooth like our skin would be and the color was a medium gray."

His hands and arms were behind his back, and he kept walking back and forth behind a little desk area. There was a chair for him to sit on and he did sit down later on. But, I never did see his hands, so I don't know how many fingers he had. His clothes were civilian clothes, but I never did see his feet because he was behind the desk area and I could only see from his knees up".

In The Room Were Anonymous's Boss and the Tour guiding Colonel "Jim" and three CIA Guys"

"My boss asked the Being what he was doing here, and why do you come here? The only answer he got was. 'We are not here to conquer the earth. We're not here to destroy anything. We are here to add knowledge to humans and so we can gain knowledge from different areas.'" Anonymous's boss told Anonymous that they definitely weren't hearing a thing through their ears and that the voice more or less they heard was right in the mind itself. And that they could put their fingers in their ears and they would still hear the being—one agent tried that. He plugged both ears to see if he could still hear the Being and he could. His boss said that the voice almost sounded like an electronically reproduced voice.

Anonymous Continues...

"They didn't tell us why he was kept there, or how long he had been there or anything like that. They basically said that they could not talk about that. My boss said that the military really didn't consider the Beings like a threat. That we don't know for sure, but we don't think that they are going to be harmful to us, but we don't really know for sure. We can't say for sure that they are not trying to invade or maybe checking us all out and especially our military bases. Because, even at that time, the saucer sightings were almost always around classified areas and at various military installations.

So it looked like they were scouting us."

Government Cover-Up

When asked, Anonymous said that the government did not refer to the beings as extraterrestrials, most of the time, but just called them the 'Grays'. He went on to say that he would have thought the government would have already informed the public about the visitations. He explained that at that time the Cold War was going on, back in the 1950', and that the CIA had a lot of cases regarding the UFOs and he went on to say that the CIA had been contacted by the Russians and that the two governments had compared notes in regard to the visitors. (Note: many in depth researchers have come to the conclusion that one of the reasons for the end of the cold war was because Reagan and Gorbachev discussed the UFO matters and decided that we should cooperate rather than be adversaries since we had visitors from somewhere else to contend with) Anonymous went on to say that the United States tried to show cooperation with the Russians by actually giving them particle beam weapons to be able to shoot down any of the saucer craft. (Note: This information is in the public record, the part about the beam weapons not the part about the craft)

One of the Most Interesting Statements

One of the most significant pieces of information conveyed in these interviews was Anonymous's firsthand account of seeing CIA files that related to a United States mission to Antarctica under Admiral Byrd code named Operation High Jump in 1946-1947.

Anonymous relates, "We had military interaction there with Aliens and their saucer craft, like a mini-war. We lost all of our aircraft." The question to Anonymous then became what did the documents, that he had access to, say, which type of pilots were engaged in battling the US Army: Airforce, German pilots or the six fingered type of beings that were revealed in the autopsies he saw?

Anonymous: "We didn't capture anything and never shot down anything, so we had no idea who was flying the saucers, except there were references to the Nazis. It was after the end of WW II that we had the altercation. The British had come up with photographs of the saucer craft in the 1930's, and so we knew the Germans had the saucer craft with 'Laser Guns' on them. Hitler actually sent most of the craft that they had to Argentina and Antarctica apparently to make sure when he started WW II none of them would be captured. Hitler always mentioned his top secret weapons and everyone thought it was the V-2 rockets, but it appears the V-2 rockets were only a side show to the saucer technology being developed.

USAF Project Bluebook Facts

From 1947 until December 1969, the United States Air Force actively investigated reports and sightings of unidentified flying saucers. UFOs, under a program called Project Blue Book. The project which was headquartered at Wright Paterson AFB was terminated in December of 1969 after 22 years. US Air Force Secretary Robert C. Seamons, Jr. terminated the project because the US Air force could no longer justify the project for national security reasons or scientific study. After closing Project Blue Book the US Air Force has not publicly acknowledged any further interest in UFO sightings.

There was no evidence indicating that sightings categorized as `unidentified' were extra-terrestrial vehicles.

Project Blue Book investigated 12, 618 UFO sightings and 701 of those sightings remained unidentified. Many UFO researchers feel that the investigators of the UFO sightings were unprofessional and unscientific. The program used poor research methods and researchers were too eager to label mysterious sightings as unidentified phenomena.

Individual researchers and UFO organizations believe that members of Project Blue Book were pressured to 'identify' UFOs sightings to calm the public hysteria about UFOs. This theory has been supported by the recent release of CIA documents pertaining to UFOs. They also suggest that any report that was never included in Project Blue book. They allege that these reports were passed on to a higher authority that never reported the results to the public.

Protect Blue Book, it seems, was just a low level collection and disinformation program created under Project Sign (of December 1947) which evolved into Project Grudge (of December 1948) to cover up the true investigation into the alien presence on Earth.

The death knell for Project Bluebook was heard in April, 1966, when the House Armed Services Committee recommended that the Air force contract with a University for a scientific study of UFOs.

On October 7, 1966, the Air force announced that a program to study
UFOs would be conducted the University of Colorado and headed
by Dr. Edward Condon. It reality the Condon committee, as it was
called, had one task, and that was to provide a reason for the Air
force to end its official investigation of UFOs.

A speech given at the Corning Glass Works by Dr. Condon soon after
the study began is revealing:

"It is my inclination right now to recommend that the government
get out of this business. My attitude right now is that there nothing to
it."....but I'm not supposed to reach a conclusion for another year.

That final conclusion of the 'Condon report', released 9 January, 1969
was:

Our general conclusion is that nothing has come from the study of
UFOs in the past 20 years that has added to scientific knowledge.
Careful consideration of the record, as it is available to us, leads us
to conclude that further intensive study of UFOs probably cannot be
justified in the expectation that science will be advanced thereby.

On December 17, 1969, Project bluebook was closed and the veil of
secrecy that had been completely drawn around wherever investigation of UFOs was being conducted by the military.

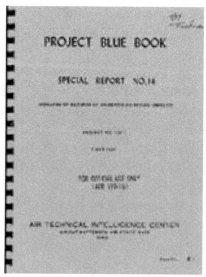

Edward U. Condon (1902-1974) was a nuclear physicist and
a pioneer in quantum mechanics who for a short time during
World War II was a part of the Manhattan Project. He was a
target of the House UnAmerican Activities Committee dueing
the McCarthy period in the US but later was made director of a
UFO Project in Boulder Colorodo ultimately called the Condon
Committee.

Section One

Area 51 Whistle Blowers

This is an interview with an army CIA UFO analyst who performed his work with Top Secret White House Clearance. The time frame was from 1957-1960. This was the "Secret Project Blue Book Files," that he was privy to. Some of the items covered in the interview:

- He states that he personally was shown 16 mm black and white film of a real alien autopsy from Fort Belvoir, Virginia. It very nearly resembled the "Alien Autopsy TV Special" that was shown in the late 1990s
- He and the other CIA agents were taken to Area 51 to interrogate an extraterrestrial person that the US Secret Government had in captivity at that most secure facility.
- The reason for the program was to familiarize our agents in the FBI and other intelligence agencies to better evaluate data that was brought to them to differentiate between hoaxed or mistaken data from the real information that the government had on them.
- He actually briefed both President Eisenhower and Vice President Nixon as to his activities.
- The agent code named "Anonymous" and "Kewper" also explains that at Area 51 he saw between 7-10 German Nazi fully operational disks. German code names were "Vril" for the smaller craft and "Hannebu" type I, II, III, IV for larger craft.
- Much more information about secret programs that he had knowledge of through the years.

Interview with Army CIA Analyst: "Anonymous"

In 1997 long time UFO researcher, Disclosure Activist, Ron Garner, Stargate Productions Producer, made contact with the family of a potential Whistle Blower code names "Anonymous"/ "Kewper". Subsequent arrangements were made for a secret interview by long time UFO researcher and author Linda Moutlon Howe. Ron Garner introduced "Anonymous" "Kewper"to Linda for the exact purpose to have the interview broadcast which would offer some measure of protection to the CIA agent who was threatened if he ever divulged his story to anyone. Linda went to his home and stayed for three days to record the interview.

The following includes a verbatim written transcript of the relevant audio tapes made by Howe of the three days she spent with Anonymous, then referred to by Garner as agent "Anonymous"and his family in their Florida home.

Because of the death threats suffered by "Anonymous"/ "Kewper", including threats to his family if he were to disclose this most secret information he discovered while working for the CIA in 1958-59 we all thought it prudent to withhold too much publicity until after the Principle's second security oath expired in 2010. To Linda's credit she did air part of the audio tapes to Art Bell on his Coast to Coast radio show on June 6, 1998. (Interviewer: Linda MoutIton Howe - Interview date: June 29, 1998

A DVD including exerpts of this interview is available through the website www.area51thetruth.com.

The principle was concerned with certain aspects of his original interview and requested that C. Ronald Garner make certain modifications to the written transcript which the principle felt would give him and his a family a little more security because his superiors demanded he not disclose certain facts. His request has been honored.

One of the Most Important Interviews Ever Recorded. Names are fictitious.

Interview with Government Whistle Blower— "Anonymous"

When You Got Your White House Top Secret Clearance At The Request Of Your Boss Jeffery Wright. (Not His Real Name) Do You Remember What Month And Year That Was?

Yes, that was end of June 1958

After Receiving The Clearance What Is The Next Thing That Happened?

We started getting fed material from Project Blue Book. I mean the real one that the CIA operation channeled through Langley and Ft. Belvoir, Virginia.

How Did It Work? You Are In The Eastern Military Base. You Are Teaching Cryptography And Signal Corps Radio Operations.

Right.

What Did Jeffery Wright Do? How Did He Handle His Parallel Life For The Central Intelligence Agency's Blue Book File?

By the middle of July 1958, I was through with my last NATO group that I taught. There were still other teachers instructing local troops, but I went on to the CIA Project Blue Book in mid-July 1958. And by mid-August, my boss Jeffery Wright and I packed up and took the trip to Area 51 in Nevada.

By Then, You Had Screened The 16 MM Black And White Film That Showed The Autopsy Of The 6-Fingered, 6 Toed Entities?

Yes.

And You Saw The Italian Photograph Of Landed "Saucer" And Small, Non-Humans?

The very first international case that came to our desk, by special classified messenger, after I started with Jeffery Wright's unit, was a photograph of a UFO from Italy. It came to us from Ft. Belvoir, Virginia, with the analysis that the film negative was not doctored and they found no trace of double exposure of any kind and declared it authentic.
The Ft. Belvoir photograph from Italy, that our CIA unit investigated, showed a saucer-shaped craft that had landed. There were two or three small, non-humans outside, like walking around. I don't know if they were looking at the plants and soil or what. These were small aliens, probably only about three feet tall. The photo was a distance away, so you could not see any facial features on the aliens. There was a kind of unusual shape underneath, round globes.

Was It A Color Photograph?

No, it was black and white. It was a small photograph like you would take with an old style Brownie Kodak camera.

What did the Craft Look Like In The Photo?

It was a silver - colored disc.

What Was The Shape?

Round. It had a small raised area on top of the disc. There were a few out-croppings on the bottom.

Do you mean metallic?

Yes, on the bottom. Almost like warts on the thing down from the bottom. The Photo was published in an Italian Magazine and someone took the photo to an American embassy and someone there in turn sent it to probably the FBI and the FBI probably sent it to Project Blue Book and from there, it was sent to Ft. Belvoir, Virginia. Since it was foreign, the photograph was sent to us in the CIA at the Project Blue Book unit in the eastern military base.

All Foreign Technology Matters Went Through Ft. Belvoir, Virginia?

Yes, everything that was not explainable. Project Blue Book first had a group of civilians and officers who would contact eyewitnesses. When a foreign case came in, they didn't have a way to contact international foreigners to check it out. So, such a case and paperwork would automatically go to Ft. Belvoir and on to us.
This is if it was something that could not be debunked—real photographs like we were shown at Area 51 in August 1958, taken from jet airplanes and Super Sabres. After WWII, instead of gun turrets on them, a lot of Super Sabres had cameras. By flying to the general area where there were frequent UFO sightings, this one group of three pilots in F100s (Super Sabres), they were following half a dozen different saucer craft to get close-up photos. But when the jets got near the saucer craft, the craft would just dart away. At Area 51, we were told it was like entering the Indianapolis 500 (car race) with an old Model-T as far as our jets trying to keep up with the saucers. Ours could not! All of a sudden, the saucer craft would zip around and be BEHIND the jets, like playing cat and mouse games.

Meaning The Saucers Could Hop Behind The Jets Before The Jets Could Even Maneuver?

Yes. Even now, my son-in-law recently told me about one of his military friends who once flew with a group of F100s that had cameras mounted and the jets flew right up through a group of saucer craft. The saucers veered off in all directions. The jets were trying to get close to the saucers to photograph, but the jets could not even get close.

[Editor' Note: F100 Super Sabres were the first mass produced aircraft capable of routine Mach 1 plus speed in straight and level flight. The prototype for this century series aircraft first flew in May 1953, while the initial production example an F100a took to the sky later that year in October-Development of the aircraft was a priority at the time due to the Korean

Peninsula troubles. The aircraft entered USAF service proper in September the following year.]

Did Jeffery Wright Give You Any Background Information About The CIA Knowing About Other Similar UFO Landings Where Beings Collected Samples?

He did give us a briefing, but it was mostly about the CIA's problem of separating real photographs from hoaxed photographs. He had some other genuine photographs of disc craft that had been taken by fighter jet cameras. Among the foreign photos he had, there were some from Mexico and Central America. Most of those were aerial photos of a saucer in the air, nothing landed. It took quite awhile to get a photograph like a landed craft with aliens outside.

Small, Gray Non-Humans Linked to Incas

Do You Remember Another Such Photo?

I remember one was from northern Mexico taken by a Mexican geologist who was out looking for oil and he had a camera to take photos of the terrain. He photographed a saucer and our CIA group compared it to the Italian saucer. Jeffery Wright said, 'These sure don't look the same.' The Mexico saucer had a big dome in the middle of it that stood up probably ten to twelve feet above the disc. That saucer craft, according to the hilly environment around it, was quite a bit larger than the craft in the Italian photograph.

Did Jeffery Wright Give You Any Background Information About The CIA Knowing About Other Similar UFO Landings Where Beings Collected Samples?

Yes, He had gone to CIA headquarters at Langley, Virginia, and then on to Ft. Belvoir, Virginia, where need-to-know people showed Jeffery Wright whatever they had so he would have a better overview. We only had the team that could go to Italy to investigate, but it was tough because those CIA people had tremendous cover in order to infiltrate governments and it was hard for us to contact them directly for discussions or to get such field CIA people to help us investigate UFO eases.

In 1958 the CIA had At Least Two Non-Human Categories: 6-Fingered Humanoids and "Grays"

In 1958, What Did Ft. Belvoir, Tell Wright About The Differences In The Various Craft?

Just that there were different types and sizes of craft and at least two different types of aliens. One was the Roswell type, the smaller humanoid that had 6 fingers and 6 toes. The other was the large head alien with big eyes and pointed chin and could be three feet tall or five feet tall.

What Did Jeffery Wright Say About The Taller One?

He said that the military referred to both sizes as "Grays" because of the gray skin color. At that time, Jeffery Wright asked where the Grays were from and the people at CIA in Langley, Virginia, told him that they had no knowledge of actual origin. Jeffery was told there were tremendous discrepancies. The Grays that had been captured, as a result of-crashes , telepathically gave numerous different stories as to where they were from. So, the CIA did not really know where the Grays were from but they thought it was outside our solar system.

Gray Non-Humans from Aldebaran Solar System?

One location the CIA wondered about was a planet described as orbiting the star, Aldebaran. There were supposed to be two planets circling that star and the Grays might come from there. Aldebaran also comes up in the German Vril Society's description that they were supposed to have contact with tall, pale skinned beings from the Aldebaran system that taught the VRIL SOCIETY how to build round craft that could neutralize gravity. (And according Admiral Byrd a similar craft could fly pole to pole at great speed!!)

Visibility

[Editor's Note: Aldebaran is one of the easiest stars to find in the night sky. It is in the constelation Taurus. It can be found by following Orion's belt from left to right in the Northern Hemisphere or right to left in the Southern Hemisphere. It is the first bright star to be found by following that line and it follows the Pleides star cluster.
Aldebaran is also alleged by the original German Vril Society of the 1920s to be the origin of space beings that taught the Vril Society how to build anti-gravity saucer craft. The Vril Society was the mother of the Nazi party. "Vril "in German means light force. The mystery persists about the Vril Society's origin and description of beings from Aldebaran teaching the disc technology. (See: Joseph P. Farrell's book "The S.S. Brotherhood of the Bell"]

Did Jeffery Wright Ever Mention Zeta Reticuli 1 And 2?

No, but he did say something about the Pleiades, a star group. It was amazing to me that the different beings, or Grays, could actually 'speak' English telepathically.

[Editor's note: Others in the human abduction syndrome have frequently mentioned Zeta Reticulii 1 and 2, 37.5 light-years from Earth, as being the home system of the Gray entities.]

But Others Exposed In Military And Intelligence Work Have Told Me It Is A Manipulation Of The Language Center Of The Human Brain. Any Person On Earth Speaking Any Language Could Be Telepathically Communicated With By Grays Interacting With The Individual Brain's Language Center.

Yes.

Jeffery Wright Met Army Lt. General Arthur Trudeau

Did Jeffery Wright Go To CIA Headquarters In Langley To Have His Own Orientation About The Ufo Phenomena?

He went to Langley first for a general meeting and I think he met Lt. General Arthur Trudeau. He was the General involved with Area 51 and technology things. General Trudeau was one of those in the meeting along with several CIA top civilians Jeffery met there.

We're Talking About Eleven Years After The Alleged Roswell Crashes. Jeffery Wright Had Served In The Oss During World War Ii, And By 1958 Was Adminstrator Of A Crytography School In The Eastern Military Base That Covered Up The Top Secret CIA Project Blue Investigations Of Non-Human Craft And Beings. Certainly The CIA Would Have Briefed Him On Everything The CIA Knew At That Time-Right?

It's possible that Jeffery Wright held some information back from us in our unit. He told us back at the eastern military base: "If we get enough of these craft shot down and capture these beings and they talk to us, we'll certainly know if there is such a thing as Extraterrestrial life out there." Not long after he said that, we got the notice to go to Area 51, in mid-august 1958. He went to church every Sunday and he was raised with the idea that Earth was the only place where there was life in the universe. But when he finally interviewed the being at Area 51, he came out and said to me, 'I think they made a believer out of me!' This thing is not human, is not part of our human race and has to be from a different solar system somewhere.'

His general comment about that—which might have been his cover-up in the context of Strict Need-To-Know security—he said all the aliens he knew about, that included the 6-fingered humanoids and the Grays that were 3 feet tall and 5 feet tall, telepathically communicated they were here to help and teach and had come in earlier centuries to the Earth. Wright said that one of the types had gone to the Inca Empire and was the one that taught the Incas how to smelt gold.

Which Alien Type?

The little 3-foot-tall Grays with the big heads, slanted large eyes and pointed chin.

The Smaller Grays Went To The Incas?

Yes.

And Taught The Incas The Smelting Of Gold?

Yes.

Why?

I don't know. He said the smelting of gold was the big thing the small Grays taught the Incas—at least that's what Jeffery Wright understood from telepathic communication.

Jeffery told me the small gray, non-humans lived for a long time. He also said that knowledge could be transferred from a dying or dead non-human into a replacement body.

From Which Captured Being Did The CIA Get That Information?

The 3-foot-tall Grays.

How Did The Alien Know?

It apparently was saying he and the other beings with him had actually taught the Incas, so that would make that alien communicating with us, very old, centuries old.

Did Jeffery Wright Comment About That?

Yes, Jeffery told me the small gray, non-human lived for a long time. He also said that knowledge could be transferred from a dying or dead non-human into a replacement body.

Had Jeffery Wright Received A Briefing At CIA Headquarters About The Cloning And The Replacement Bodies?

No, Don't think so. I don't remember him mentioning cloning, but he said the replacement bodies and very long lives of the non-humans were brought up in meetings at the CIA. These things either live a thousand years/ or their knowledge can be transferred to a new body unit if their body wears out.

Did Jeffery Wright Refer To Their Bodies As Androids?

No. At that time even when we went to Area 51 in August 1958, the being there in that office building was described as being extraterrestrial. At that time with us, we also never heard the phrase, 'extraterrestrial biological entity (EBE). The particular term was never brought out to us. It was the term 'alien' that was always used as the all-encompassing word to describe the beings. At that time, apparently, our government thought they were in-dependent beings from somewhere else in the universe—not programmed androids working for someone else.

Not much is known about the 6-fingered non-humans

If Jeffery Wright Had A Briefing In Which It Was Explained That The 3-Foot Tall Grays Had Been Involved With Teachng The Incas About The Smelting Of Gold, Was There Also A Briefing About The 6-Fingered Hu-manoids?

No. I had the impression that there was no detailed knowledge about the 6-fingered, 6-toed entities, what they were up to or why they were here. All I ever heard was that the Grays were here to help and had helped different nations do different things over the centuries.I never heard anything about why the 6-fingered beings were different from the Grays and I never heard any information about where the 6-fingered aliens were from.

What About The Taller 5-Foot-Grays?

I understood they were from the same solar system, but a different planet. But at that time in the late 1950s, only the planet Aldebaran was mentioned to me as a possible source. I don't know.

The Only Star That Jeffery Wright Brought Up In The 'Eastern Military Base Was Aldebaran?

Yes.

No Other?

At that time, no other. When we were at Area 51 in August 1958, some other stars were mentioned, but I cannot remember what, except they were identified only by numbers, not names.

Electromagnetic, Anti-Propulsion And Anti-Matter Propulsion Systems

In What Jeffery Wright Learned At Langley CIA Is There Anything More About The Types Of Beings And Craft Technology That He Talked To You About?

Yes, he mentioned that there was one type of propulsion system that was electromagnetic anti-gravitational. Also, they had some other craft that operated on a different type of anti-matter propulsion system, which was quite a different type of propulsion system altogether. Also, they had found one ancient saucer craft that was atomic powered and was still highly radio-active. It had been put into a cave out west in the United States and when there was an earthquake, somewhere, the side of a mountain tumbled down and exposed this radioactive craft sitting in a cave. It was atomic powered. Our government investigations had no idea about the age of it but thought it was much older than anything else they had found.

[Editor's Note: In a recorded interview with another major whistleblower— Bill Uhouse—He stated that the "Aliens" had a serious interest in an important, rather rare, Earth mineral - Boron]

Extraterrestrial Uranium. Mining in Europe.

Jeffery Wright told us that in Europe they had found a place where, long ago, someone had mined uranium, but the mining went back maybe 50,000 years or some really ancient time. In the uranium mine, there was no sign of picks and shovels because the walls of the mine had been very precisely removed by some kind of cutting tool that removed the uranium.

Uranium. Mines Have Been Found Where Governments Concluded Non-

Human Aliens Had Done The Work Centuries Before?

Yes, and the discoverers followed where the uranium ore had been cut out and it was the highest quality uranium. The sub-quality mineral was just left. The modern human miners then mined what was left of the lower quality stuff. The discoverers said they thought the smooth, carved tunnels in the high quality uranium had been done thousands of years ago.

Jeffrey Wright Has A Briefing And He Must Have Said Something To You About The Relationship Of The Past Alien Interaction On Earth And Why There Is Interaction Now?

I believe he asked a similar question to his briefers at Langley and the answer was a run around that they didn't know, but they thought the aliens had been here for many hundreds or thousands of years before. The difference between our modern times and ancient times is now we have fast communication between towns and nations. Back when humans lived in small villages, the aliens could operate around the planet however they wanted because from one village to another , there was little communication about their activities.

So, Why Would The Non-Humans Be Here Now?

Jeffery Wright, said his briefers stressed they did not know why. The answer they gave him was that the aliens said they had come before as helpers of humanity and that's the only answer he got from anyone.

Did Anyone Bring Up German Technology?

No, he never heard of any German WW II technology until I found the documents in the CIA library.

Ok, That Was In July 1958 When Jeffery Wright Had Come To The CIA For A Briefing With Some CIA Colleagues About The Aliens. He Comes Back To The Eastern Military Base And Has A Session With You And How Many Of Your Colleagues?

There was just the two of us, Jeffery Wright and me—we were the only two with Top Secret White House clearance. The other men just had Top Secret and there were three of them.

So A Total Of Five Of You Altogether - As An Inner Group-Studying The Highly Classified CIA Project Blue Book Files?

Yes. We were in a larger group of 26 men, including Jeffery Wright, rang-
ing from Florida to other CIA units beyond our school and Top Secret Blue
Book stuff.

*So, Five Of You Are In A Room And Jeffery Wright Briefs You About What He
Learns? What Happens Next?*

He gives me and three others the message that we are going to Area 51 to
see some of the craft there because we had to make a report on it when
Jeffery and I went to the White House. Jeffery said that since we in the CIA
unit were working on the international UFO situation and would be receiving more and more of the foreign photographs and other materials, the
Langley CIA headquarters wanted to have some of us fly to Area 51 to see
some of the craft there hauled in from various places; and in two weeks we
would travel there (mid-August 1958)
By then, I was teaching a Signal Corps training course for new instructors
and refreshing others and had to finish my class work. Then we flew to Area
51 in mid-August 1958

Screening the 6-Fingered, 6 Toed Autopsy/Dissection Film, July 1958.

*So What Happened For You To See The Autopsy/Dissection Film Of The Six
Fingered, 6 Toed Beings?*

The dissection film was shown to us before Jeffery Wright went to Langley.

So You Had The Italian Photo And Mexican Photos—What Happened To
Lead To The Screening Of The Film Of The 6-Fingered Alien?

[Editor's Note: Lt Col Phillip Corso stated that he had also seen an autopsy
film similar to Anonymous's description.]

Jeffery Wright received a message that a package with a Top Secret classification had been delivered to him and it was a film of an alien autopsy. There
really was no sound to it other than a narration introduction saying the
autopsy was done shortly after the craft was recovered and some was done
in the clinic in the town or Roswell and some of the film was done at the
Army Base near Roswell.

*Go Back To The Day Of The Screening And Tell Me How It Was Organized.
Was Jeffery Wright There To Talk About It?*

He only had a printed report that came with the film. He had no idea the film was coming until it was there.

So, Your Boss In Charge Of The Project Blue Book Unit In The .eastern Military Base Has You And Others Go To A Screening Of A Non-Human Autopsy In What Kind Of A Room?

It was the top floor of a two story classroom type of building in the classified section of the base known as Cryptography 722. It ws fenced in by huge fences that had barbed wire on the top. The place was manned with armed guards and gun turrets and if anyone tried to climb over the fence the guards would shoot them. We had some KGB agents that tried to break in and a number of them were shot trying to get in.

All That Force Protection Was In Place At The Army Base For What Reason?

Because it was the CIA headquarters base for the eastern United States. But other highly classified cryptography schools in the United States also had manned guards. And once we had the CIA Project Blue Book there, then we had something that was highly, highly classified beyond normal CIA activities that included information about CIA field agents that was highly sensitive information. We didn't want any Soviet spy to get any information about our CIA field agents. We had a number in Cuba, for example, and they would have been killed if Castro learned they were agents.

What Time Of The Day In July 1958 Did You Gather In The Classified Building To Screen The Non-Human Dissection Film?

It was about 10 AM and all the doors were locked in the building.

You Had No Idea What You Were About To Screen?

No, no idea.

How Did People Get Into The Classified Section Of The Building?

You had to go through the gate and the gate had M.P.s there. Also, we all had weapons that we carried and they checked our weapons permits we carried with our CIA identifications. But we did not have to check our weapons at the gate; security wanted to make certain each of us was authorized to carry the weapon we had. I had been issued a Luger pistol with a silencer for when I began teaching the Asiatic classes. We were armed because we were concerned that Communists in the group might try to kill us

In 1958, Was A Metal Detector Used Or Any Electronic Technology For Fingerprints?

They had no electronic fingerprint scanning, but when we entered the building, they had our photograph with fingerprints there to compare.

When You Got To The Room, Were There Guards At That Door?

There was a guard outside the door and there were two guards at the gate when we first came in. Once we were in the building and on the second floor for the meeting there was no more checking. And my boss, Jeffery Wright, was downstairs on the first floor and told each of us to go up to the second floor. He knew each of us and he counted everyone going to the room for the screening. There wee twenty-six of us counting Jeffery Wright. Once we got to the second floor room, all the window shades were drawn and a couple of big fans were going. We could not open any windows and there was no air conditioning, so it was about 110-degree F. temperature up there at the time. I remember sitting there with sweat running down my back.

What Were The Screening Facilities Like In That Room? Who Handled The Film?

Jeffery Wright handled the projector and we had a white screen that pulled down in front of the blackboard that was on the front wall of the room. It was a motion picture screen we would normally use to show films during our 722 Cryptography classes. Jeffery already had the dissection film in the projector ready to go when we got into the classroom. Jeffery Wright told us it was going to be a special film of aliens (non-humans) and it was the aliens that crashed in New Mexico who were dissected. He didn't say specifically Roswell.
Later on, he told me it was the Roswell, New Mexico crash. He didn't tell the whole group for some reason.

How Did He Define The Roswell Crash To You?

After the autopsy film, he asked me if I had read about the Roswell, New Mexico, UFO crash. I said I remembered it well because I listened to the radio and saw newspaper explanations about it being a weather balloon. Jeffery Wright said it was NOT a weather balloon. It was an alien crash in New Mexico. I asked him which crash because I had heard about other crashes. He said it was the Roswell crash. I asked him why he did not tell the whole group that the 6-fingered beings were from the Roswell, New Mexico crash?

Jeffery Wright told me those were instructions in the report and correspondence that came in the Top Secret classified package that contained the film. He was to say only that the beings were picked up in New Mexico.

On the film itself, when there was a narrator's voice that gave a verbal lead into it, the narrator mentioned that the alien autopsy/dissection took place in the hangar at the Army/Air Force hangar near Roswell and that some of the body dissections took place in a clinic that was in Roswell itself.

There Still Was No Identifier On The Film About The Specific Location From Where The Beings Were Retrieved?

No. There was nothing in the audio narration and nothing specific in the printed text of the narration we were given to read as well. The few photographs of the bodies in addition to the autopsy were photographed in a hangar at the Army Air Field near Roswell.

Did Jeffery Wright Ever Have Specific Knowledge About Where The 6-Fingered Non-Human Bodies Were Retrieved?

Yes, from Roswell.

But Was It The Craft Between Corona And Roswell, The Trinity Site At White Sands, The Plains Of San Agustin, Capitan Mountain Or East Of Alamogordo Or Any Other Place? Roswell, As An Army Air Force Base, Would Have Been Used In A Generic Way For Any Crash In The Region. Did He Know Exactly Where The Bodies Had Been Retrieved?

He said these were the ones from the early July 1947 crash from the first saucer craft. I asked him what type of craft and propulsion system it was. Jeffery said he had no information at all and hoped that in two weeks when we went to Area 51 that someone would give us more details.

Jeffery Wright stood up in the front of the room and said we were going to see a film that had just been sent to us (CIA unit) that it was received that morning and was the reason for that particular meeting. It was a film of aliens that were picked up after a crash in New Mexico and this was an autopsy film and this would be our first view for any of us as far as a film of this type of alien. Jeffery said it was very important and for us to get a good image in our minds of what this type of alien looked like so if we saw photographs come into our unit of aliens that looked like this, we would know about this particular type of alien.

Jeffery Wright - Sits Down Next To The Projector And Begins To Project The Film. In Your Mind's Eye Now, Can You Recall What The First Scenes Were?"

"After the medical people cut off the top of the skull,
you could see two brain hemispheres, but instead of having a solid brain like humans, it looked like a lot of branches.We called those alien 'branch brains."
"Anonymous" Former Army/CIA UFO Analyst

The film started with an introduction and there was wording on there too, so if you had a projector that didn't pick up sound, you could read what the narrator was saying. It was a very short introduction and started with showing some alien bodies just laying on wood pallets, That is what it looked like.

How Many Were There?

There were three bodies.

Any Clothing?

No, just in their bare skin, I guess you would say. First, we saw one that was—you could recognize it like the one in the alien autopsy because it had a damaged leg. He had his head turned sideways and it looked like he had some kind of injury to the skull.
When they started the autopsy, we could recognize the three we saw on the wood pallets in the hangar, although this might not have been all of them because I believe there were four beings in that crash.

Did You Ever See All Four?

No.

In The Film When It Started, You Could See Three Beings On ...

Wooden pallets like you would put boxes on but these didn't have spaces like some pallets. These had solid wood on top.

As If Something Had Been Put Together Just To Put Those Bodies On To Be Filmed?

The pallets were probably something they already had and just happened to use the pallets to put the alien bodies on, I would think, because in the military you have lots of pallets for forklifts to put boxes and stuff on. Pallets are only a few inches thick from the ground and most have only strips of wood going across them and are hollow in between. But the pallets the aliens were laying on had solid tops, which would be normally used to pile on smaller boxes.

Was The Camera Angle Looking Down On The Bodies?

Actually from the side. You had the one, two, three bodies and you're looking across them at a slight angle down.

How Far Was The Camera From The Bodies?

From the first one, probably about five feet. And there was one body slightly higher up on the pallet and then the third one. So. I guess 5 or 6 feet from the first body and the pallets were about 3 feet, so the pallets were fairly close together, so the end alien body was probably 8 or 10 feet away.

How Long Were The Pallets?

At least 6 feet long. The bodies were laying kind of centered in the pallets and had about a foot and a half at each end that was not covered.

So You Think The Beings Were Only 3 Feet Tall?

Yes, I would think so—3 feet to 3.5 feet tall, somewhere in there.

Was There Any Information Given In The Film About The Heights Of The Beings?

Absolutely nothing in the film itself. It only said they were 'small, alien beings.' When we looked at them, we noticed right away that they had six fingers. We couldn't count the, toes because the feet were together. But it mentioned in the write up that Jeffery Wright received that the beings had six fingers and six toes.

So, He Did Have That In Writing?

That was in his typed pages of what was in the film.

So That Is Why You Paid Attention To The Number Of Fingers And Toes?

Yes. Jeffery mentioned that in the rundown: small aliens. I think he said 3 to 3.5 feet tall and that they had six fingers and six toes.

In The Written Paper, Did It Say Anything About Internal Organs?

It did mention about the autopsy that we would see that none of the internal organs are the same as ours.

Anything About Pathology Results?

Yes, all three of them had pathology results.

{Editor's Note: "Autopsy Report: The Anatomy of the Aliens" as told by Dr. Dan Burisch/Crain microbiologist is featured in another DVD found on www.area51thetruth.com that corroborates this by his experience with a live Extraterrestrial at Area 51 as well as seeing a similar autopsy film to the one that Agent Anonymous viewed at CIA Headquarters]

Unfortunately, that was about it. But when you cut open a human chest, you would see the lungs. But in that general area of the beings in the autopsy film, there was a large organ in that area they cut out and put it in a stainless steel pan. It did not look like our lungs.

Did The Three Bodies Have Raised Stomachs?

Yes, all three of them did.

Opening The Non-Human SKULL

"...instead of having a solid brain like humans, it looked like a lot of branch-es. We called those aliens 'branch brains' "
                          Agent Anonymous

In The Dissection/Autopsy Film, Did They Show From The Beginning To The End Of The First Cutting And Conclusion?

Yes, including opening up the skull and exposing the brain. The body was opened up first and then the brain and the head—they cut around the head with some kind of device used to cut the skull open. Then they took the top of the skull right off and showed the brain structure. The brain structure was not like ours. Our brain structure is very compact and solid. If you hold up a human brain, you have the two hemispheres. After the medical people, cut off the top of the skull, you could see two brain hemispheres, but instead of having a solid brain like humans, it looked like a lot of branches. We called those alien 'branch brains.' " This is what the guys called them. There were little strips coming out with all these little brain nodules on the strips and they had two precise lobes, the right and left. But they were not solid - sort of like broccoli.

Discrepancies Between 6-Fingered Alien Autopsy Film Anonymous Screened in July 1958 and the 1995 Santilli 6-Fingered Autopsy

In The 1995 Dissection Film That Was Broadcast On Tv, When They Took Tissue Out Of That Entity's Skull And Put It In A Metal Pan, It Looked Dark, Sort Of Like Liver?

No, that's something completely different. In the autopsy film, we saw with Jeffery Wright, the medical people did not take the brain completely out of the body.

The Bodies Were The Same In The Film You Saw And The Santilli Tv Broadcast?

The bodies were the same, but if the brain came out like a big piece of liver, it was not the same brain that we saw. The doctors had cut the skull right above the alien's eyebrows and took the entire top of his skull right off.

When You Saw The Bone Being Lifted Off, What Was The First Thing You Saw When They Lifted Off The Top Of The Skull?

The brain structure. It looked like a bunch of main stems coming up from the front and going across the back, but they were distinct structures like little twig branches with lobes coming off from them in all directions.

You Could See A Vertical Branch And See Branches Coming Off The Main Branch?

Yes, and little lobes on the branches and we were all laughing about it afterward calling them 'branch brains.'

This Was Black And White Film?

Yes

And What Color Would The Branches Have Been On A Gray Scale?

I would say they were dark gray, not black. They were hemispheres like our brain is right and left. But they were not solid like ours.

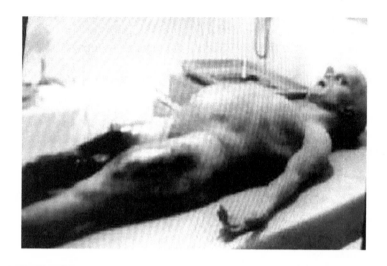

Section Two:

- The Interview Continues Regarding The Autopsy At Walter Reed Hospital
- Discrepencies Between The Film Anonymous Saw And The Film Shown On Television By Santilli
- More About The Non-Human Brain
- A Visit To Area 51
- Camouflaged Office Complex And Disc Hangar At Papoose Mountain
- CIA File About Roswell, New Mexico, Alien Crash

How Many People Were Doing The Surgery?

Two, and it was amazing because they had long, white, regular surgical gowns on, but when one of the doctors turned around, I noticed there was a monogram on his sleeve that was 'WR.' I asked Jeffery Wright about that, did he notice the monogram? Doctors don't normally monogram their surgical garbs and it looked like a stamped `WR.' And Jeffery Wright said, `WR . Oh, that's Walter Reed.'
I asked,'Why would this doctor be wearing a Walter Reed hospital gown.' Jeffery said the doctors were flown out to Roswell from Walter Reed.

[Editor's Note: Walter Reed Army Medical Center (1909-present)is located at 6900 Georgia Avenue N. W., Washington, D. C. 20307]

So, Your Boss Accepted That The Dissection/Autopsy Was Done In Roswell?

Yes.

As Opposed To The Bodies Being Flown To Walter Reed? Wouldn't It Have

That was probably done at the Roswell Army Air base. But the second part of the film that showed the actual autopsies, they said it had all been done the same day. However, when they showed the film in the hangar of the three bodies, before his camera panned around to film the bodies, you could see it was bright sunlight with a couple of little fluffy clouds in the sky. You could see right outside.

You Mean The Cameraman Was At First Pointing The Camera Through The Hangar Door To Outside?

Right, he started filming on the sunny daylight outside and panned around to the three aliens on the pallets in the hangar at the air base outside of Roswell.

Now, when we saw the film of the autopsy, it was in a solid room. But one time they were filming in a different direction and you could look out a small window. A portion of the top of the window was not covered with a curtain and you could see real gray skies. Even though they said everything had been done the same day, I think it's likely that's not true and that the alien bodies were taken somewhere else for the autopsies.

But Nobody Said That?

No. I asked Jeffery Wright about that and he said, 'This is all I have.' I told him about the sunny sky with white clouds versus the gray sky and. how could all of it had been done the same day. It was a really dingy gray sky in the autopsy film.

What Did Jeffery Wright Say To Your Observation?

He said, 'You're pretty sharp and you might have something there.' I also told him we saw three alien bodies there and maybe one was air-lifted to Walter Reed Hospital where they had a lot of expert medical doctors that were trying to get as much knowledge from the being as possible rather than having a local Roswell doctor do the autopsy.

Been Easier To Fly The Bodies To Walter Reed?

I feel that the lead in on the film, the beings laying on the pallets—yes,

In Jeffery Wright's Description And In The Words On The Film, Was The Word 'Extraterrestrial' Ever Used?

No, just 'alien.'
In Terms Of The Three Bodies, Was The Wide Shot From The Camera In The Hangar The Only Wide Shot You Saw Of The Three Bodies At One Time?

Yes.

In That Wide Shot, Do You Remember Any Differences Between The Three Bodies?

One seemed slightly smaller than the other two. But generally, they were the same in appearance.

More Discrepancies

Were The Eyes Open Or Closed As They Lay There On The Pallets?

I believe all three had their eyes open. They were large eyes, but not like the huge eyes depicted on the Gray beings. The eyes were larger and had bigger pupils than human eyes. But generally the overall appearance was like a small person.
The eyes had whites around the iris/pupil like we have. They were five feet away and we couldn't distinguish much more about it than that of the three laying there.
Even in the one laying on the autopsy table, I remember seeing eyes that were a little larger than human eyes.

In The 1995 Dissection Film (Santilli), It Showed The Removal Of Black Lenses From The 6-Fingered Being's Eyes. Is That What You Saw?

No, we saw nothing like that. Nothing like black lenses, no. I didn't see anything like that.

So You Are Describing A Different Film?

Yes, I realize that now. I didn't realize that when I saw it on television in

1995. I thought that was the same film we saw at the military base.

But You Are Remembering From Your Own Screening Of The Bodies Laying On The Pallets, You Did Not Have The Impression Of Solid Black Eyes?

No.

Autopsy Sequence in Film Anonymous Saw

In The Dissection Film That Jeffery Wright Showed You, Can You Remember The Surgery Sequence?

They started by opening up the throat area and came down opening it up all the way down to the belly area. Then there were a couple of cross sections so they could peel the body back to get at the internal organs. They took the big organ in the chest first that did not look like lungs. It was sort of a rectangular mass, all in one unit. They took that out and put that in a shiny stainless steel pan.

When You Say A Rectangular Mass, Do You Mean Like A Pound Of Butter?

No, not that long, but it was definitely not square. It was longer than it was wide.

But You Mean The Large Internal Organ Removed From The Chest Area Was Rectangular In Shape?.

Yes, it was the first one they took out from the chest—or what we would think of as the lung area. It was a large organ that was held in two hands and put into the metal pan. I also remember seeing there was no intestinal tract like we have looping around. There was nothing like that. Then the doctor started taking out smaller organs, different types and shapes."

Could You See The Face Of The Being Clearly During The Autopsy?

No, not really, because when they had cut the throat, they had pushed the face kind of back and they had the camera down fairly low showing the chest. You could see the bottom of the face, but I think that was all.

Before They Started To Do The Cutting, Did They Show A Close-Up On The Non-Human Face?

No, the only close-up on the face was when they were cutting the skull. They had the face at an angle at that time as they were cutting around with the mechanism they used to saw through the skull.

Could You See The Eye?

Yes, and it was a large eye with white or light gray around the eye. But I never saw anything in the autopsy film we were shown at the eastern military base that looked like black lenses over the eyes.

What Exactly Is The Same In The Photos I Have From The Santilli Broadcast Compared To What You Saw In The Autopsy Film In July 1958?

The size of the body, the muscle structure, the ears, the shape of the face and head. But no solid black eyes (or lenses).

Surgery Room Is Different in Film Anonymous Saw

Are You Seeing Any Image That You Remember Specifically From The Autopsy Film You Saw?

The table structure is different in the Santilli images compared to what we were shown. The Santilli images show the knives and cutting things in a different place. In the film I saw, the tray was up against the wall and there definitely was no telephone like you see hanging on the wall in the Santilli film. The surgeon (in autopsy film screened at eastern military base) had a tray behind him with all kinds of cutting tools on it, a tray on wheels.

Did You See Any Images In The Autopsy Film You Screened That Focused Close-Ups On The 6-Fingered Hand And 6-Toed Foot, As In The Santilli Film And Photos?

The hand with the six fingers looks familiar, but I don't recall the surgeon holding up the hand to designate the six fingers. When I counted the fingers in the autopsy film that we saw, the arm was just laying down like this (flat on table). I don't remember the surgeon's hands near the fingers and toes.

Was There Anything That Definitely Stated Four Beings Had Been retrieved?

[Editors Note: Other information not from Anonymous says the fourth being was found alive and that's why only three bodies were lying on the wooden palette, including one with a badly damaged right leg.]

I believe, if I remember correctly, that Jeffery Wright told us there were four bodies. But I read through the film instructions after the meeting and it did not state how many bodies. I asked Jeffery and he said that when he was at the Langley facility in the early spring or summer when they told him he would be doing this autopsy screening, they went over some material at that time that showed him details about the Roswell crash and there were four beings. But we only saw three in the autopsy film.

In The Film You Screened, Did You See The Dissection/Autopsy Of Only One Being?

Yes, only one.

So, Everything You Saw And Everything That's Been On TV Could Be Valid, Done In Different Locations At Different Times?

Yes.

But What Is Puzzling, If There Were Black Lenses Over The Alien Eyes— Which Even Lt. Col. Philip J. Corso Said He Had Information About—Why Would The Black Lenses Be Off The Eyes Of The Three Beings Lying On The Palette In The Aircraft Hangar?

That's hard to say. It could be that someone had already removed them for an unknown reason to study them.

Did You Have The Impression That July 1947 Was The First Retrieval Of The Four Beings?

Yes, I did. That might not be true, but Jeffery Wright and I thought these were the first beings picked up and that other ones (Grays?) came later the same year or another year.

Non-Humans With Protruding Bellies

In The Autopsy Film You Saw, After They Opened Up The Chest And Re- moved That First Large Organ, Do You Remember What They Showed Or Removed From The Distended Belly Area?

There was nothing that resembled intestines at all. It was just a bunch of smaller organs. One looked a little bit like our kidneys, only a little wider and bigger. But there was nothing there that I saw in 1958 that really resembled 100% any human organs of any kind.

Do You Remember Anything Under The Protruding Belly?

No. I remember when the surgeon opened it up, he started taking out different organs, differently shaped organs. Nothing stands out specifically.

No Round Thing Right Underneath The Surface Of The Protruding Belly? That Round Organ Is Definitely In The Santilli Dissection Autopsy Film That Was Broadcast On TV?

No, I don't remember any round organ in the belly.

No Sexual Organs—Are the Beings Cloned?

Did They Show Any Gynecological Examinations In The Slit Opening Of Any Of The Beings In The Area We Would Consider To Be A Pubic Region? (Santilli Had Film Allegedly Of Exam.)

No, nothing along that line at all. They just said they could not tell (sex differences) Jeffery Wright said in the introduction that they could not tell if they were male or female in the three beings.

Do You Remember Anything That Resembled White Tendrils?

What do you mean tendrils?

Something That Would Be Very White In The Black And White Film That Has White Tendrils Coming Off It?

No, I don't remember anything like that.

Was There Any Mention Of Belly Buttons Or Lack Of Belly Buttons?

Nothing was mentioned that I recall.

There Were No Belly Buttons On The Beings In The Santilli Film In 1995, Which Implied That The Beings Were Cloned.

Oh!

Did They Show In The Autopsy Film That You Saw Any Examination Of The Leg Wound?

No. But I did see a leg wound in the right leg (like Santilli photos).

Was It A Wide Shot Before The Autopsy In The Film You Saw?

No, the only wide shot we saw was the three beings lying on the pallets.

Did You See A Wounded Leg Anywhere Else In The Film?

No.

Just In That Wide Shot?

Yes. I saw one of them had the wounded leg and the other ones did not.

Did You Ever See The Surgeons Take Out Of The Non-Human Bodies Any Organ Or Object That Resembled A Thimble?

A thimble? No.

[Editor's Note: Santilli film shows unidentified thimble-shaped object during dissection/autopsy.]

Were There Any Shots In The Autopsy That Showed Anyone Else In The Room Besides The Two Surgeons Working On The Autopsy/Dissection?

When there was a change to the shot that showed the window in the door that showed a dark gray sky, they had a clock on the wall that was kind of a square, wooden clock with a good sized frame around it. I didn't see any cords coming down. I remember that on the wall.

No Cords?

The clock was on the left hand wall. In the side view when I saw the window, I could see one of the doctors at that time and he was facing the camera more (the other doctor was facing another angle), but he had a mask on his face and some kind of thing around his head, so the only thing you could see were his eyes.

Protective Glasses?

Yes, I think he did have glasses on. 1 don't know if they were protective glasses. But they looked like thick glasses like maybe he had bad eyesight or something.

Or They Were Being Used To Magnify During The Autopsy Procedure?

More About Non-Human Brain

After Cutting The Being Open And Lifting Out The Various Organs, Did The Procedure. Then Switch To The Brain?

Yes. I don't remember them taking everything out of the being, but they took a lot of organs out of the abdomen area and around it, but it seems like there was something left in there. And then they started on the head. And just above his eyebrows is where they cut his head all the way around and opened up the skull. When they opened the skullcap up, it did not look as thick as our human skulls. Human skulls are pretty thick and it was not that thick. But the skull cap itself when they sat it down on the edge of the table. It could stand by itself and was still a skullcap, so it was thick enough for that.

Then You're Looking At The Branches With Lobes That Were More Of A Gray Color And Not Black Or Dark In The Black And White Motion Picture Film?

Yes.

What Did The Surgeons Do? Did They Cut Out A Lobe Or Branches?

No. They held the opened head toward the camera so you could see the two hemispheres of the brain. But they did not take the brain out of the skull. They left the brain where it was. Then they made another cut down by the ear like they were trying to see the inner ear. Maybe in respect to the eye so they could see from the brain to the eye as far as the visual connection in the brain - something like that.

Was There Any Sound At All?

No, no sound whatsoever.

So, Silent Film. Do You Have Any Memory Of The Last Scenes On The Film You Saw?

It was the scalp being cut off and the surgeons holding up the head so we could see the two brain hemispheres. Then they started cutting by the ear and toward the eye and inspecting with little instruments of some kind, kind of probing through the brain. It looked like they were trying to see how the brain was connected to the eyes and ears. Basically that was the end of the autopsy film we saw.

Was The Film Going And Then Just Stopped?

Yeah, the camera kind of zoomed back real fast and was shut off. That was it. There was no wording on the end as far as explaining anything.

After The Film Ran Out Of The Projector, What Did Jeffery Wright Do?

He said, 'Well, this is it. This is the first time I've seen this."

What Was His Reaction?

He said that he was surprised at the brain and at the internal organs and that the beings were neither male nor female.
He asked me, 'Anonymous, how do you think they, reproduce?' And I said, on top of a Xerox machine!' (laughs)

Did Wright Ever Have More Information From The CIA. Or Anyone Else About The 6-Fingered Beings?

No, not a thing.

Did Any Of The Film You Saw Show Any Of The Craft, Or Pieces Of Craft?

No, nothing about the craft.

What Did Wright Say After That? The Film Was Shown, There Are 26 Men. Were They Asking Questions?

Yes, they were all asking questions. Since Jeffery Wright and the film introduction described them as 'aliens,' the audience reaction was, 'Well, they sure look like us in miniature form.' One guy in the back of the room said, 'Wow, the aliens have bigger stomachs than Anonymous!' (laughs)

You've Always Had A Bigger Stomach?

Yes, a protruding stomach. They used to tease me about that.

What Did Jeffery Wright Say To The Group?

He said that the explanation at the front of the film was the only information we had, other than this was sent to our group to view and in two weeks, five of us would be going to Area 51 in Nevada and probably would get further information at that time. Jeffery said if that did happen, he would call together the rest of the group after we returned to give further information - unless it's classified Top Secret White House.

In Those Next Two Weeks, Did You Get Together With Jeffery Wright Over Coffee Or A Beer To Talk With Him?

Yes, a couple of time we got together for lunch. During those two weeks, I was teaching an instructor training class and trying to improve our instructors we had because they were floundering. I was busy at that, but we did meet twice and talked about the fact that I was completely baffled, completely puzzled as to what these beings could be since the information listed them as 'aliens' on the paperwork. Jeffery Wright told me he hoped we would find out more when we got to Area 51.

Trip to Area 51, Nellis AFB, August 1958

Ok, Two Weeks Later, What Was The Process To Get You To Area 51? The Group Is You, Jeffery Wright, And The Three Men From Your Italian Photo Analysis Team?

Yes, we knew two weeks in advance when we would be leaving and where we would be leaving from. MP's picked us up in a van at the headquarters parking lot and then took a total of five of us out to a military plane at the local largest airport. The military plane was ready to go and we climbed on board with just a little bit of luggage. Each of us had one small suitcase. No cameras. No guns. We had to leave our guns at home. I always felt naked without my gun.

Were You Ordered Not To Take Notes Or Audio Recordings?

Right, no phones, no recordings, no notes—just what we saw visually and heard while we went through the Area 51 tour.

Now You're In August 1958 And You Fly To?

Flew to the air base in Nevada.

Directly To Nellis AFB?

Yes, we were able to get there without stopping.

You Landed On The Base?

Yes.

Who Was There To Meet You?

The Col. "Jim" with only the one-name nametag. I knew his name was phony, too, because a couple of times I said. "Jim" and he didn't answer me right away like he wasn't used to recognizing the name.

Was He In Professional Military Uniform?

Yes, not dress blues, but regular USAF military uniform with the Colonel badge and his hat and the scrambled eggs on the bill, the whole thing.

Was The Van Already There With The Colonel When You Landed?

Yes, he was there with a little shuttle bus, which was a Ford shuttle van. After we landed the pilot drove the plane around to a place to park it. Then portable stairs were put up to the plane and we got off. Col. Jim was right there and the van was then waiting for us and we went first to the main hangar building at the airport. There. Col. Jim gave us a little briefing that we were going out to the classified area where they have some equipment such as the Blackbird and some of the U-2s. He said, 'You've probably all heard about U-2s. Well, we've got a couple of those here.'

[Editor's Note: Wikipedia - "The Lockheed U-2 (U for 'utility') is a single-engine, high-altitude aircraft flown by the United States Air Force and previously flown by the Central Intelligence Agency. In the early 1950s, with Cold War tensions on the rise, the U.S. military required better strategic reconnaissance to help determine Soviet capabilities and intentions. The existing surveillance aircraft were primarily converted bombers, vulnerable to anti-aircraft artillery, missiles, and fighters. It was thought an aircraft that could fly at 70,000 feet (21,000 m) would be beyond the reach of Soviet fighters, missiles, and even radar. This would allow 'overflights' knowingly violating a country's airspace to take aerial photographs. After a meeting with President Eisenhower, Lockheed received a $22.5 million contract for the first 20 aircraft. The first flight occurred at the Groom Lake test site, also known as Area 51, on August 1, 1955, during what was only intended to be a high-speed taxi run. The sailplane-like wings were so efficient that the aircraft jumped into the air at 70 knots (130 km/h).”]

"You're going to see some highly classified equipment.
At this time, we have some saucer craft that have been gathered in the United States from New Mexico and we have other craft that have been gathered from around the world."
- "Col. Jim," USAF, Area 51, Nevada

Then Col. Jim said we were going out to another area to cover some highly classified projects and material. So we went roughly eight miles to the first hangar area. We went inside the hangar and saw a Blackbird. Then we saw a couple of U-2s. They were working on one of them. They had the engine apart on one and were loading cameras into the other one.They had U-2s there because, as I understood, Area 51 was setting them up for a special photography run of some kind. The Blackbird was new and highly classified then.

Was It Replacing What The U-2S Had Been Doing?

Yes, it was a replacement plane for the U-2s.

Jeffery Wright Had Not Seen A Blackbird Either?

No, he had not. The Blackbird was brand new to us.

You Are On A Tour To See Classified Stuff, But No One Has Said To You, 'We're Showing You The Blackbird And U-2S Because We're Using Them To Monitor Alien Activity On Earth?

No. nothing to that effect. It was just that the U-2s would-be used for a special project and the Blackbird was there because it was in the highly protected area. The general public had never seen the Blackbird before. When it was flown at night, no one could see what it looked like.
We knew that the U-2s had been used to fly over North Korea during the Korean War for high altitude spy shots. Nothing was said about the U-2s or Blackbird being used to get photographs of alien saucers or other. Col. Jim described some of the Blackbird's advantages in high speed and that it could fly higher than the U-2 did. The U-2 had an engine, I think, with just 6,000 pounds of thrust. The Blackbird had two engines with around 20,000 pounds of thrust and it could refuel in the air.

More Travel to See Disc Craft and Gray Entity

Do You Remember Anything About How Col. Jim Handled The Next Phase Of Your Tour To The Ufo Craft And The Gray Being?

After we left the hangar and got back on the van bus, Col. Jim told us it was about eight miles to the next area where we were going to visit and see more highly classified material and aircraft there. We said to each other, 'Well, we just saw the Blackbird! How highly more classified could you get?'
We guessed we might see a saucer vehicle that might have been picked up at Roswell or some place like that, but we didn't really know until we walked into the 'cave' hangar area that we were going to actually see some, which we did.

You're All Together In The Van And Col. Jim Is With You?

Yes, he is with us all the time. He is in the front seat and we are further back. The van was one of those 12-passenger vans.

While You Are Traveling Those Eight Miles, Is Col. Jim Talking To Anybody?

Somewhat, but the van was very noisy and had no air conditioning. It was really dusty and the windows were down along the side for ventilation. The wind was blowing, so it was hard to hear. We did ask him a few questions, but not very much because we really could not hear him.

Camouflaged Office Complex and Disc Hangar At Papoose Mountain

What Did You See Through The Front Van Window When You Came. To A Stop?

We saw ahead of us some buildings that looked like they could be hangars and some office buildings.

What Was The Shape And Height Of The Hills?

They called them 'mountains,' but they were a little low to be classified as real mountains. They were probably 3,000 to 4.000 feet high -- not the type of mountains that snow would be on. More accurately, they were large hills.

Where Did You Pull Up First In The Van?

An office complex area. We got off the van and Col. Jim told us we were going into the office complex first He said there were things in there he wanted to show us. So, we got off and went into the first office complex. There was office personnel working there. You could see one guy making copies at a Xerox machine and an older woman was filing stuff in a filing cabinet. There was a kind of reception area, a nice room that had a TV in it if you were waiting for something. I never did understand why they had an open reception area with a TV because you could hardly get in there with a tank! Even Congressmen don't visit there! The only people who can visit have to have very high security clearances with Need- to -Know. Maybe the reception room was for Generals and people like that.

Is The Complex Right Against The Mountain?

Yes, the office complex rests against the mountain with some buildings going right up to the mountain edge. Then you have a fairly steep cliff area and you could see sort of an arch in the mountain stone. It's not an open arch, but that's the area that had a cave in the bottom of it and the military had taken rock out of this cave and enlarged the cave into a hangar.

So You Think It Was A Naturally Existing Cave That Was Modified?

Yes, it was made much larger, but the initial main hangar cave was probably already there.

Were There Connecting Ramps And Stairs That Went From The Office Complex Directly Into The Cave Hangar?

There was just a little short walkway about five to six feet with a roof over it and you walked through that right into the cave hangar. The cave hangar just had this one narrow entrance area from the office complex and everything was rock around that. When we went in the entrance way and I looked back and all I could see was rock everywhere. Then further on as we viewed the saucer craft, you could see a larger doorway where they brought the craft through.

What Do You Think A Satellite Would Have Seen Of The Cave Hangar?

Satellite would have seen nothing probably.

What About The The Office Complex?

There was slight camouflage on some of the buildings that tapered down

onto the edge of the mountain cliff area where they had camouflaged netting going across the building roof closest to the cliff. That was the only
camouflage I saw. The other hangar type buildings they had out there,
which we didn't go into, looked very flimsy and temporary. They weren't
well built.

What Was Inside Of Those?

We never learned about them. We went out the back way and the van met
us there and we never did get into the flimsy structures. We had no idea
what in those.
We went into the cave hangar from the office complex. Col. Jim said,
`You're going to see some highly classified equipment. At this time, we have
some saucer craft that have been gathered in the the United States from
New Mexico and we have other craft that have been gathered from around
the world.' Then he took us through a small doorway and there was a curve
in the hall. We went into the main hangar area and there was a roped off
walkway along the edge of the hangar. He took us right down the roped off
walkway. We could not get close to the craft.

*Is It Built So The Natural Cave Is Forming The Wall Of One Of The Office
Complexes?*

Yes, one building was built right against the wall of the cave, not touching
because you would have water running down the mountainside area when
it rained. If you had it too close, you would have water in the building. But
the wall was within a foot or two at least of the cliff wall. That building had
the camouflaged netting draped over it.

On That Camouflage Netting, Was There Sand And Rocks?

No, it looked like regular military camouflage, like something you would
throw over a tank to camouflage it.

How Does Only Netting Camouflage?

You have brown and green colors and it's close netting. From an aerial view,
it looks like a continuation of ground. The short walkway from the office
building took us right into the cave entrance. From there, we went in a
smaller little cave room and then a sharp right to go through an area that
has about an 8 or 10 foot opening. After that is a walkway and to the left is
the whole bay of chiseled out natural cave where the saucer craft were.

It Was All Hard Rock Wall, Ceiling And Floor?

If I remember correctly, something had been done with the floor to level it. There was some kind of a poured cement floor. There were some areas that looked like a flat cave floor, but most of it had cement poured in to make it level. We are walking along the edge of the right hand wall of the cave.

How Far Are You From The Closest Craft?

I'd say about thirty feet.

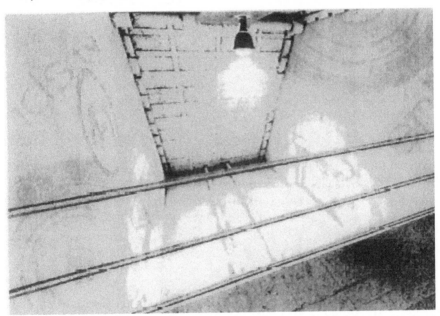

"There were main hanger bays and catwalks that I with five other CIA agents traversed in 1958 to view the various disc craft that were stored there at the time.

At Area 51 the first craft we saw looked identical. They were not like the ones in the back. Col Jim mentioned that those two were "Vril craft." We asked him what Vril was, he said it was a foreign saucer build in germany in the 1920's and 1930's. Then he pointed up ahead and said that certain saucer shaped craft were alien (extraterrestrial) craft retrieved from New Mexico. There were three more in the rear, huge, all sitting on metal saw horses or stands to keep them off the ground. The disk on the very back part was very impressive and Col. Jim said that it was a German WWII craft built in 1938 and was jacked up higher on stands showing a gun emplacement underneath, which he said the Germans called a 'death ray.' It was different than the other craft, was dark in color, and had a larger top that stood up probably 10 or 12 feet above the center and it had a diameter of about 50 or 60 feet.

[Editors Note: Nazi-Disc-Photos.html reports: The SS E-IV (Entwichlungsstelle 4). a unit of the SS Occult Order of the Black Sun was tasked with researching alternative energies to make the Third Reigh independent of scarece fuel oil. Their work included developing alternative energies and fuels.

This group allegedly developed by 1939 a revolutionary electro-magnetic gravitic engine an improved Hans Coler's free energy machine into an energy converter coupled to a van- type generator and Marconi vortex dynamo (a spherical tank of mercury) to create powerful electromagnetic fields that affected gravity and reduced mass. It was designated the Thule (Thrustwork, aka Tachyonator-7 drive) and was to be installed into a Thule-designed Pioneered by SS metallurgists specifically for both the Haunebu and Vril series of discs. With some new kind of metal and Haunebu I had a double hull of an even more exotic metal called Victalen.

The early model's also attempted to test out a rather large experimental gun installation-the twin 60 mm KSK (KraftStrahiKanone, Strong Ray Cannon) which operated off Triebwerk for power. It has been suggested that the ray from this weapon made it a laser, but it was not. The Germans called it an 'anachronism' gun-not belonging to that time period or out of place.

When a Vril 7 was downed by the Russians in 1945, a similar underbelly mounted KSK type canon was destroyed and eventually recovered from the battle site. Postwar, the strange metal balls and the adjacent spirals that made up the weapon could not be identified. But recently it has been speculated that the Triebwerk-connected balls formed cascade oscillators that were connected to a large shrouded transmission rod wrapped in a precision tungsten spiral, or coil to transmit a particular burst suitable to pierce up to 4 inches (100 millimeters) of enemy armor. The heavy gun created problems and badly destabilized the disc. See: http://www.roswellufomuseum.com/research/ufotopics/naziufocrash.html]

At area 51, the craft described by Col. Jim as Vril, were not shiny silver. It almost looked like some kind of coating, or fabric-covered, because there was no shininess. Maybe the metal was deteriorating after twenty years of being stored, this was 1958."

VRIL 7 craft in 1947 Source Rob Arndt

You Had Never Heard Of A German Disc Before Then?

Well. on our first trip to Washington D.C. when we were with Jeffery Wright we were in the CIA headquarters and we looked at files and saw some documents about Germany at the end of World War II.

What Date Did You Make That Trip With Wright ?

In May or June 1958. That was shortly before our CIA group, in the eastern U.S. Military had been sent the first UFO photographs. Jeffery Wright and I went to Langley. It was supposed to be at the White House briefing.

You Mean To Talk With The President?

Yes, and the President was Dwight D, Eisenhower and the Vice President was Richard M. Nixon. We were instructed to show them the Italian photos and other UFO photos at that point.
We were supposed to talk with VicePresident Nixon first and the CIA was then going to do the special Project Blue Book briefing but that meeting never materialized.
We were scheduled for the first meeting at Langley, CIA headquarters, in Virginia. The rest of the trip was cancelled. I don't know if it was because Nixon had to fly somewhere. But something happened to him, so we did our own research in the CIA archive.

Were You Going To Meet Vice President Nixon There?

-No, we were going to the White House in the Oval Office. That's where we met three times after the appointment was cancelled.

After 1958?

Yes.

Had Jeffery Wright Met With Nixon Before?

Yes he had, Jeffery was in the White House with some CIA officials just shortly after Eisenhower was elected in January 1953.

Related To The Disc Phenomena?

No, I don't think so.

So, On This Trip Around June 1958 You And Jeffery Wright Were Supposed To Meet With Vice President Richard Nixon About The Disc Technology?

Yes, Eisenhower and Nixon knew all about Area 51 and what was going on with the aliens. Of course Harry S. Truman knew all about it, too. But I think Nixon and Eisenhower were the last two presidents to know everything. As far as I know, John F. Kennedy did not know much about it, at least that is what Wright's son told me later presidents were just chopped off from the Need-to-Know after Eisenhower had been given highly classified alien information.

Did Wright Tell You Why You Were Supposed To Have A Meeting With Vice President Nixon?

It was in regard to our organizing the CIA unit to analyze foreign UFO photographs, We were with the agents that were tasked to try to debunk some of the reports. As counterintelligence agents we were supposed to talk with Nixon first about how he planned to handle the foreign films and photographs.

Because You Would Be Trespassing International Boundries And Negative Consequences For The U.S. Being In Other Countries If Agents Got Caught?

Yes, It was always a very tricky thing. Even the agent in Mexico had to get affiliates who were briefed about the order to do interviews of eye witnesses and photographs because he was so tied up with the Media officials he could not get free to go into the field to do the work himself.

So, you're At CIA Headquarters In Langley, Virgina, And The Meeting Was Cancelled, Who Suggests You Go To The CIA Archive Files?

My boss, Jeffery Wright, had been in the archive library before to see if there were any boxes that had been sent to the CIA for storage that might contain UFO photos and films. So we looked.

CIA File About Roswell, New Mexico, Alien Crash

What Did It Look Like And What Was The First Thing You Saw?

The first thing I read was a form about Roswell. It was four pages stapled together and it was a description of the Roswell craft after they had been recovered on trucks and where they went. It said was craft was taken to the air force base outside of Roswell for the first day. Then, on the second or third day they were taken to to Ft. Riley, Kansas and they wre headed for Dayton, Ohio.

Why Ft. Riley?

Ft. Riley is an Army training center and the Roswell Craft went there as a stopover en route probably only a couple of people, or no one, knew what was in the truck or trucks parked overnight.

This Was En Route To Wright-Paterson AFB?

As I remember, it was destined for some place out side Dayton, Ohio, and then I think it went to Wright Paterson AFB after that. I'm not certain what happened in Dayton, Ohio, but it stopped at some small bivouac area then it went to Wright-Paterson where there was already either a classified area---or they built a clandestine hanger because the craft would be kept there. At least one craft was there for some time, for months, and then it went to California to a smaller air force base out there. Not Edwards AFB. It was another smaller base I don't remember the name.
Then apparently it went to Area 51 for awhile. They hauled it around to different scientists that had the clearances from WWII working on various projects and had the scientist look at the craft to see what they recognized and what functions the craft had.

[Editor's Note: The Grandson of an Operation Paper Clip German Scientist sent to Wright Patterson Airbase to examine the metal of the craft told his Grandson when he was a child that the metal was not of this world. His Grandson did not understand the significance of this revelation until a friend's father asked if the family still had the Grandfather's scientific notebooks. He had been studying his work and confirmed the information and the Scientist's credibility.]

Were There Any Photographs Of The Roswell Craft In That File That You Looked At While At Langley?

No, I didn't see any. It could have been already taken out because the file was eleven years old then (June 1958). There was a lot of blacking out censorship on a lot of the forms and names of officers who were there during the retrieval were all blacked out. Just their ranks were given.

CIA Document About Roswell Describes Craft as Crescent-Shaped, Not Disk

Was There Any Physical Descriiption Of The Craft?

They had a description that it was crescent-shaped and it had one or two small, horizontal stabilizers on it. One had been completely torn off. I know that's quite a bit different from the saucer shaped generally associated with the craft; the sketch in the file was crescent shaped. But no information on the sketch about when or where it was taken from. But it was in the file labeled Roswell

Anonymous Saw CIA Documents about "Aliens" Transported with July 1947 Recovered Craft to Ohio Via Ft. Riley Kansas

Was There Anything In The Files Written Documensts About The Six Fingered Humanoids?

Very little—only that they had found some dead aliens and one was still alive and was in some kind of a unit. a hand-held unit with a little hose on it that he plugged into his suit. The being had some kind of breathing device and that the being was having labored breathing.

Did He Say Anything About Where The Live Being Went?

No, it just said the live alien was taken away. I mentioned that the three dead ones were picked up and put in containers, probably preserving chemical like formaldehyde. And placed in plastic coffins like for children's bodies—something like that. But authorities were able to seal the containers with the dead bodies completely submerged in the preservative liquid in see through plastic containers.

But It Did Not Say Where The Bodies Went?

Well they went with the craft on the truck that first went to Ft. Riley, Kansas. It also mentioned that the bodies were sent for autopsy to find out more about the beings. It did not say were they were taken. I suppose to various places.

In The File, Was There Any Mention Of The Plains Of St. Augustine?

No, not in that particular file. That was just the Roswell file and there was nothing special in the paperwork. It just mentioned some miscellaneous paperwork annotations filed by the military that had originally picked the craft up.
There was a notation about the cover-up - that the second day, a cover- up story about the wired deflectors hanging down from the balloon. That was listed as a cover story to cover up finding the crashed saucer.

Did It Say Anything About Why There was A Decision To Cover It Up?

It mentioned that the decision to cover it all up came from the White House, the very top, so that it was President Truman's decision to cover it up. I would think.

But No Explanation?

No, there was nothing much about the recovered live alien and the three dead aliens. There were no reports of ET beings or of the autopsies or any thing. When there are excuses - that files have been destroyed, like the file Jeffery Wright and I saw at Langley it is probably in the same envelope right now labeled various Miscellaneous Notes.

Like They Were Filing Sensitive Subjects Under Common Innocious Categories To Keep People From Stumbling On To The Material.

That's right, and you can imagine a huge warehouse a half a block long, you could be there a month looking through boxes looking for something.

In an excerpt from "The Day After Roswell," Retired Colonel then Major Philip J. Corso describes how one day he was making his rounds at Ft. Riley when he came to the the veterinary building where a soldier named Brown was supposed to be standing watch. When he got there he didn't see him and knew that something was wrong.

"Brownie" as he was called was supposed to be outside the building , not hiding in the doorway where he was eventually found. It was a breach of duty.   ["You don't understand, Major, you have to see this." Better be good," I said as I walked over to where he was standing.
"The guys who off-loaded those deuce-and-a halfs,"he said. "They told us they brought these boxes up from Fort Bliss from some accident out in New Mexico."
"Yeah, so what?" I was getting impatient with this.
"Well, they told us it was all top secret but they looked inside anyway. Everybody down there did when they were loading the trucks. MPs were walking around with sidearms and even the officers were standing guard," Borwn said.
"But the guys who loaded the trucks said they looked inside the boxes and couldn't believe what they saw. You got security clearance, Major. You can come in here."
In fact, I was the post duty officer and could go anywhere I wanted during the watch. So I walked inside the old veterinary building, the medical dispensary for the cavalry horses before the first World War, and saw where the cargo from the convoy had been stacked up.

"What is all this stuff?" I asked.
"That's just it, Major, nobody knows," he said. "The drivers told us it came from a plane crash out in the desert somewhere around the 509th. But when they looked inside, it was nothing like anyting they'd seen before. Nothing from this planet."
Then Major Corso saw thirty or so wooden crates nailed shut and stacked together. He found one that he was able to open.
"I picked up the top and slid it off to the edge. Then I lowered the flashlight, looked inside , and my stomach rolled right up into my throat and I almost became sick right then and there.
Whatever they'd crated this way, it was a coffin, but not like any coffin I'd seen before. The contents, enclosed in a thick glass container,were submerged in a thick light blue liquid , almost as heavy as a gelling solution of diesel fuel. But the obect was floating, actually suspended, and not sitting on the bottom with a fluid over top, and it was soft and shiny as the underbelly of a fish.

At first I thought it was a dead child they were shipping somewhere. But this was no child. It was a four-foot human-shaped figure with arms, bizarre-looking four fingered hands-I didn't see a thumb-thin legs and feet, and an oversized incandescent lightbulb-shaped head that looked like it was floating over a balloon gondola for a chin. I know I must have cringed at first, but then I had the urge to pull off the top of the liquid container and touch the pale gray skin. But I couldn't tell wheither it was skin because it also looked like a very thin one-piece head-to-toe fabric covering the creature;'s flesh.

Its eyeballs must have been rolled way back in its head because I couldn't see any pupils or iris or anything that resembled a human eye. But he eye sockets themselves were oversized and almond shaped and pointed down to its tiny nose"}"The Day After Roswell," pages 22-23

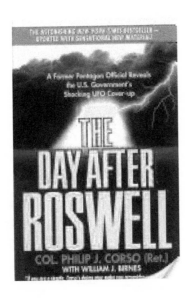

Major Philip Corso
"Day After Roswell"

Section Three:

- Interview continues... Points Discussed:
- Discussion regarding German Alien Propulsion System
- More information about the Hitler connection
- Agent explains photographs he examined of German Disks
- Agents concern about the Area 51 Non Human might be a Demon
- More discussion as to Why Nazi Vril Craft were not used in world War II
- Information regarding the US capture of some of the Nazi craft
- Six Fingered Control Panel and Headbands
- I Beam "Alien Hierographics"
- Telepathic Exchange
- Different Aerial Craft German and Interplanetary
- Drawings and photographs of German Haunebu Craft
- Alien Agendas: Human Abductions and Cattle Mutilations?
- CIA trip to brief Vice President Nixon

What Other Files Did You Look Through?

We looked through the WWII German File.

What Was That File Called"

"End of World War II Argentina File," something like that.

Did Jeffery Wright Read That File With You?

No, he was still in the Project Blue Book category. Later I went to get him and brought him to see the Roswell file and the German File. He read the German file first because he thought it was more exciting. In this particular file about the end of WWII Germany agreements, these documents were typed out with a script typewriter—script print. That's super fancy, like if you typed up an expensive will and testament document. Real nice looking. Jeffery mentioned that he had never seen script form of typing in any other documents he had ever seen. And the script did not look like it belonged there because it wasn't like government typewriters or teletypes we saw in most documents.

What Were You Reading?

It mentioned movements at the end of WWII. It mentioned tracing where Adolph Hitlerhad left. Three weeks before the final end of the war when the Germans finally surrendered, Hitler went in a small airplane to Norway, Hitler and Eva Braun both, and the burned body outsoide of the basement stronghold where Hitler had been was his double and not him. The Russians knew that and found paperwork in regards to the body double. The Russians knew that it was not Hitler who died in the bunker.

How Did People Know Hitler Had a Double?

Even at the end of the war in the last days or weeks, Hitler had all the small children those 11 through 13 – that were out shooting rifles in his youth program. There were all these little kids with rifles and the news film showed Hitler coming out of his bunker and shaking hands with the kids. Hitler told them to do the best they could because Germany 'is in your hands,' having lost a lot of soldiers. So, Hitler told the children they had to do the work of men. In those films when he went out to see the children, Hitler looked very old and decrepit, like he was very ill. The reason for that, I believe, is that Hitler's double was older than the actual Adolph Hitler.

How Old Was Hitler At The End Of World War II?

He was 56.

According to Brad Steiger and
Sherry Hansen Steiger in their
book "Real Aliens, Space Be-
ings and Creatures from Other
Worlds,"
Secret Societies in Germany
Wanted to be Found Worthy
For the Alien Masters of the
World.

[Editor's Note:
The secret societies formed in Germany in the late nineteenth and
early twentieth Centuries wanted desperately to prove themselves
worthy of the super humans that lived possibly beneath the surface of
the planet Earth or on other Star systems They also wished to be able
to control the incredibly powerful Vril force. The ancient force had
been known to the alchemists and magicians as the Chi, the Odic
force, the Orgone, the Astral Light.

In 1919, Karl Haushofer, a student of the Russian mystic George
Gurdjieff, founded the Brothers of the Light Society in Berlin and
soon changed its name to the Vril Society. The members of the Vril
Lodge believed that those who learned control of the Vril would become a master of himself, those around him and the world itself if he
should so choose. The members of the Vril Society were well aware
of the Astral Light's transformative powers creating supposedly out
of the orinary mortals. Such of the Lodge as Adolf Hitler, Heinrich
Himmler, Herman Goring, Dr. Theordor Morell (Hitler's personal
physician) and other top future Nazi leaders became obsessed with
preparing German youth to become a master race so the Lords of
Inner Earth woudl find them worthy above all others when they
emerged to evaluate the people of Earth's nations.

As Haushofer's Vril grew in prominence it united three major
occult societies, the Lords of the Black Stone, the Black Knights of
the Thule Society and the Black Sun. While the societies borrowed
some concepts and rites from theosophists, Rosicrucian's and various
Hermetic groups, they placed special emphasis on the innate mysti-
cal powers of the Aryan race.]

Hitler was known to have a body double after the atempt on his life at Valkyrie. The Russians claimed to have in their archives a divan with blood stains and a piece of human skull with a bullet hole in it. "Mystery Quest" a show on the History Channel had the skull tested for DNA and it was discovered that it belonged to a female between the ages of 20-40.

Did Anybody In Our O.S.S. (Office Of Strategic Services Was CIA Precursor) Have Actual Firsthand Eyewitness Testimony That Hitler Was Using A Double?

On some of the forms in the Germany file at CIA Langley, it said definitely that our U. S. government knew Hitler had a body double from at least the spring of 1944. It also mentioned that Hitler and Eva Braun flew in a small airplane to Norway and went from there to South America in a submarine. The only reason our OSS spies knew that Hitler was in that plane is that Hitler had special buttons on his topcoat and a Fuhrer button was found in the airplane that had ripped off his coat. He was in the backseat that had to be pushed forward in order to climb out of the airplane. Apparently that's when his button hooked on the edge of the backseat and tore off as he was getting out of the plane and was lodged right there.

In The Document You Were Reading At The CIA Langley Archive, Where Did It Say That Hitler And Eva Braun Went In The Submarine?

The file said some of the submarines went to Antarctica and some went to Argentina. But Hitler went to Columbia, South America.

It Said That In The Document That Had The Script Print?

Yes, that Hitler had a German base in southern Columbia. (Northwestern South America West of Venezuala.) The document Jeffery and I read said that Columbia is where Adolf Hitler went. Then when he arrived we in the U.S. had OSS people there who reported that Hitler had shaved off his moustache and he was very sad looking because Eva Braun died in the submarine on the way to Columbia from a ruptured appendiz.

What City In Colombia?

I don't know. The document just said southern Colombia where there was a German stronghold. The Germans had quite a bit of property in southern Colombia. There were a lot of Germans already there that escaped earlier as everything was falling apart. Most of them went to Argentina, but there were some of the upper echelon that went to southern Colombia, the big wheels like Hitler.

Was There Anything In The Document About Hitler After He Was In Colombia? You Were Reading About A 1945 Event In 1958, Which Was Only Thirteen Years After WWII Ended?

The form we were reading at the CIA archive was in a box dated 1946, and the documents were dated like the summer of 1946, I believe. It was not a 1958 document. These were older WWII documents

Was There Anything In Files Dated Later Than 1946 About Hitler?

No, the only reference in the 1946 document was about him in southern Colombia. It mentioned where he was in a German stronghold and gave coordinates about north, west and so forth about where the stronghold was exactly. The document said Hitler was getting down in Colombia *The New York Times* and the *Chicago Tribune* and the *Berlin* newspaper *after the war.* So, our OSS guys were tracking what mail Hitler was getting in Columbia.

In 1958, Did Jeffery Wright Say Anything About Finding Out More Nformation About Hitler In Columbia?

The only thing we found that was dated later was one small folder labeled '1948.' That folder is the one that mentioned that the United States had an expedition going to Antarctica with Admiral Richard Byrd. There were quite a few soldiers and a number of aircraft. Some were ships at sea. There were half a dozen ships. When they got down to Antarctica the airplanes had skis so they could land on the glacier-packed areas. So they had a sizeable force. Also there were jeeps sent down.

[Editor's Note: Admiral Richard E. Byrd, Jr. was an American naval officer who is the subject of mystery and controversy. He was a pioneer in aviation, polar exploration and claimed to reach the south and north poles by air. Although it is considered to be unsubstantiated, Anonymous confirms that Operation Highjump, a highly publicized expedition to find Nazis who fled to Antarctica at the end of World War II was mentioned in secret CIA files. The expedition was to find a secret base with submarines, aircraft and flying saucers.

What Agent Stein/Anonymous was describing was not the cover story given for Operation High Jump. Operation High Jump, which took place in Antarctica from 1946-47 was conducted by Armiral Byrd and concerned 13 vessels, 23 aircraft along with a military force of 4700 men. It was harely, "merely" a scientific expedition. A Further Historical Note: UFO conspiracy Researchers contend that a possible reason for James Forrestal's (the first Secretary of Defense) untimely death was because he had planned to go public with the real reason for Operation High Jump- Namely our involvement with left over Nazis and ET Aliens in Antarctica and all over South America.]

Did The Document Say Why Admiral Byrd Was Doing This?

The document in the CIA files said Byrd was sent to Antarctica by the US government, but the cover story was a scientific expedition to map out areas of Antarctica. It also mentioned that Byrd encountered other military forces, allegedly Nazi forces based there. The document said our troops that we sent there met strong resistance from inidentified forces there, left over nazis or aliens.

We also found information about VRIL technology. The first thing in the file when we opened it up was a British classified document which was from the 1930s before WWII started. It showed that in Peenemunde, the Germans had developed the saucer craft with an entirely different kind of propulsion system. Intelligence did not know exactly what the propulsion system was, but they knew that the craft did not burn any fossil fuels. It had a levitation device; I think is how they described it in the files.

Was there anything about Extraterrestrials in the VRIL File?

It said there were mediums who had contacted aliens and there were messages from aliens about how to build the levitation device for the anti-gravity engine.

Did Jeffery Wright See That?

Yes, and he said to me that the more we read, the more we had no idea about what had really gone on in WWII.

He was Seeing the VRIL Material For The First Time?

Yes. We were hurrying through the files looking for references about alien beings but didn't find much except a brief mention about some mediums contacting aliens concerning levitation devices.

Jeffery Wright, Who Came From The OSS And WWII And Knew So Much. What Did He Say?

We talked frankly when we got outside the CIA building. You had to watch what you said inside the CIA headquarters. We knew it was all electronically bugged.

When You Walked Outside, You Said Jeffery Wright Turned To You And Said?

'I never expected to see this. I expected to see more on aliens, but I never expected to see that WWII had so much to do with German technology. And when we saw the two saucer craft at Area 51, Jeffery looked at me then, and said, 'VRIL craft.' The third big one, with the gun on the bottom; Col. Jim also said was a VRIL craft. I saw information that some VRIL craft went back to the early 1920s.

What Was The Diameter Of The First Two Small Vril Craft?

I think about 18 to 20 feet on the VRIL craft. The middle alien craft were 30 to 40 feet in diameter and then the back craft were about 60 feet in diameter.

Ok, Try To Mentally Put Yourself On The Catwalk And And You Are Looking Out At The Craft And Try To Give More Details, Starting With The Front Two VRIL Craft.

The two front VRIL craft were almost identical. They were small, around 18 to 20 feet diameter, and looked very light.

What Was The Shape?

A little slight bubble in the center, like just enough room for one person's head. The craft sloped down around from the slight bubble. Then the next three larger craft were identified as 'alien craft.' There was one that was some 30 feet in diameter at least, maybe 35 feet.

What About Color?

The three alien craft were were all silver-colored. Those three were not identical. but reasonably the same and the biggest one had a raised dome or cabin on top.

How Are The Alien Ones Different From The VRIL?

The outcropping or cabin on top was a little bit higher on the VRIL craft, maybe 3 feet high and below on the VRIL craft. It was flat on the bottom. The alien craft had like three rounded domes on the bottom. On conventional aircraft, you might think they were radar domes, but on the bottom of the discs. These were on the bottoms of the extraterrestrial craft.

You Definitely Heard Col. Jim Tell You That The Three Discs In The Middle Were Extraterrestrial Craft?

Yes, 'alien craft.'

So There Are The Two, Dull Silvery, VRIL Craft In Front That Are About 18 To 20 Feet In Diameter. Then There Are The Three Shiny Silver, 'Alien' Craft In The Middle That Were 30 To 35 Feet In Diameter?

Yes, and one of the three alien craft a little farther back behind the front two might have been 30 feet in diameter. The three alien craft were not the same diameter. And the designs were slightly different. The largest one had a very low cabin area, but the whole craft were thicker than the other two smaller ones. The two smaller ones were thinner craft and higher center areas.

Did All Three Have The Three Rounded Domes On The Bottom?

No just the larger one.

What Was The Source Of The Alien Craft?

Col. Jim said all three were from New Mexico.

Any Specific Geographical Locations?

All col. Jim said was, 'we got these three alien craft from New Mexico.' He didn't specify a Roswell or other location. We saw one of the craft that had been dismantled in one area because it was open on one side. We could see it was open, but from where we were standing, we could not see from the back side inside. That possibly could have been one of the Roswell crashes they were studying to back engineer so they left it apart.

Did Col. Jim Say Anything Specific About The Three Alien Craft?

I asked him what the propulsion system was on the three alien craft. Col. Jim at Area 51 said the alien craft propulsion systems were anti-gravitational on two of the craft and one craft had an anti-matter type propulsion that was much more complicated. Apparently they thought that the anit-matter propulsion was older and more complicated than the newer anti-gravitational systems in the other two craft.

Beyond The Front Two VRIL Craft The Three Alien Craft In The Middle. How Many More Were There In That Papoose Mountain Cave Hangar?

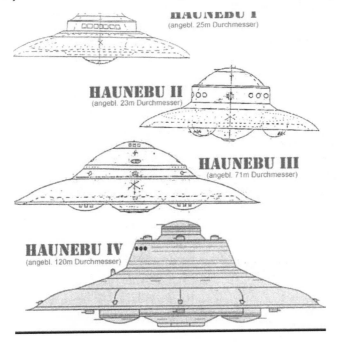

Diagrams of German craft designed in a remote location of Hauneburg. The name was shortened to Haunebu.

There were two more. One was about 50 feet in diameter and is kind of a different structure. Those craft had much larger structures protruding upward, like maybe 8 or 10 feet above the disc. And below on those, one was just aa slightly curved bottom but mostly flat. The other one also had just a curved bottom, but it had a gun emplacement of some kind hanging from it. Col. Jim said the Germans called it a 'death ray,' something they had been developing in early WWII.

Did Col. Jim Say Those Two Larger Craft In The Back Were German?

Yes, German craft and they found them, I believe, in Germany in the back of the Messerschmitt aircraft plant down in southern Germany near Austria.

So What Was Happening In Peenemunde?

In the 1930s, Germany was building the VRIL craft there. Then later on, Germany started building V-1 and V-2 rockets for a big push to attack England. All the other craft and technologies were moved away from Peenemunde and the two large discs at Area 51 had been moved to the Messerschmitt plant.

[Editor's Note: Peenemunde is a village in northeastern Germany. Shortly before and during the WWII a military center was set up at Peenemunde for developing tested guided missiles in particular the V-1 flying bomb and V-2 rocket.]

Did You Or Your Boss Ask Col. Jim- If The Germans Had Such Craft With A Ray Gun Underneath- Why Didn't Hitler Use The Death Ray In WWII?

Yes, we did ask. Col. Jim said he understood that Hitler chose not to use them, that these were the 'wonder weapons' that Mussolini and Hitler mentioned. Many people thought the German V-1, V-2 and V-3 rockets were the Nazi 'wonder weapons,' but that was not true. The discs were the wonder weapons with their speed and anti-gravitational technology.

You Were At Area 51 How Long After Your Trip With Jeffery Wright To The CIA Langley Headquarters Basement Archive?

The June 1958 Langley trip was two months before the August 1958 trip to Area 51.

And You Were Shown The Black And White 16 MM Autopsy Film At The Northeastern Military Base Two Weeks Before The Area 51 Trip?

Yes.

So After All That, After You Get To Area 51 In August 1958 And Are Standing On The Walkway With Jeffery Wright, Col. Jim And Your Three Other CIA Colleagues Did Any Of You Say, 'We've Seen The 16 Mm Film Of The Autopsy/Dissection Of The 6-Fingered Humanoid. Which One Of These Craft Belongs To Them?'

Yes, we did ask that and all Col. Jim said was, 'they told me since I've been here that these three alien craft were retrieved from New Mexico, but I don't know which one is which or exactly from where. All I know is all three area supposed to be from New Mexico.'

That Is All Col. Jim Said?

That's it.

Did He Know Where The Four VRIL-Type Craft Came From?

The other four ,Col. Jim said ,were picked up in foreign areas. He said that the German Messerschmitt Haunnebu 1 and 2 were picked up in Germany. The other smaller two VRIL craft I woudl think were picked up in Germany as well, but Col. Jim acted like he did not know where those two craft were retrieved.

In Addition To The Seven Discs, Was There Any Debris You Could See?
There was a doorway on the far end that curved and went out to other areas. There was a big double or triple door that folded open on the other end that could have been another hangar area, but we never got into that one.

[Editor's Note: Both Area 51 Whistle Blowers Microbiologist Dr. Dan Burisch/Crain and Physicist Bob Lazar describe the same type of hangars with Alien Craft stored there.]

Taken from 16mm film Alleged to be the hand panels from the ship.

6-Fingered Control Panels and Headbands

While You Were There, Did You Ever See Any Control Panels Like The Ones In The 1995 Santilli Tv Broadcast Film?

I saw control panels in drawings of them, the 6-fingered control panels.

Where Did You See The Drawings?

I saw those in the Roswell file itself at CIA Langley. I saw pictures similar to the Santilli film with the symbols on it and they had several printed pages fastened to the drawings that described how the 6-fingered panels worked with fingertip controls. The controls were tied to fibers that at first they could not identify how they worked. They saw little fibers running off to the end that plugged in and they did not know it was fiber optics because they had not been invented! In the printed pages that went with the drawings of the panels, they described 'fiber filaments.'

That's What Investigators Looked At Under A Microscope?

Yes. It described them checking at least one of the hand panels and found that all the 'fiber filaments' that we now know are fiber optics were all tied into the electrical current throughout the craft. It also said in that printed text that there were so many 'fiber filaments' in that craft that when it was picked up from the crash site, it had a slight glow to it from all the fiber optics in it. The craft glowed in the dark! The pages attached to the 6-fingered panel drawings said that all the walls of the craft glowed, everything was wired in this Roswell craft for electrical current.

When The Beings Had Their Hands Placed Into The Panels, What Happened?

Our investigators came to understand that the 6-fingered imprinted panels controlled all the craft's functioning, including the anti-gravitational device. Our investigators did not know which finger did what on the control panel, but they knew all the fingers were primary to complete control of the craft, a craft apparently entirely guided by the being's hands.

When Their Hands Were In The Panels That Were Fiber Optically Connected To The Craft, Didn't You Mention Reading About The Entire Craft Becoming A Capacitor?

On the print out that I saw in the Roswell file, the investigators did not find a distinct power plant in the Roswell craft they were studying. It was as if the entire craft provided the electromagnetic and anti-gravity fields and even the aliens that flew the craft—like their uniforms were tied right into the electronic field and maybe the aliens themselves.
Besides the 6-fingered control panels, they had pictures of the headbands that the aliens wore. With the combination of the headbands and the fingers in the panels, the aliens could guide the craft.

The Headbands Were In The Roswell File At CIA Langley?

Yes.

[Editor's Note: Lt. Col. Philip J. Corso Also Talked About Alien Headbands in his bestselling book "The Day After Roswell." In that book Lt. Col. Philip J. Corso is a former pentagon official who reveals the US government's shocking UFO cover-up. The Alien headbands are referred to on pages 98-99.]
.

The Roswell file mentioned that human pilots tried the headbands hooked up to mild electric current, but all they got out of it was violent headaches. Naturally our brains would be different from theirs and whatever caused the craft to go one way or the other for the aliens didn't work for the human brains.
We now use head bands in fighter jet helmets hooked up so when the pilot looks to the right, the guns will turn in that direction. We've had that tech-nology since the 1980s, probably back-engineered from the alien technol-

ogy.

I-Beam "Alien Hieroglyphics."

What Was The Debriefing About The 6-Fingered Humanoids? How Were They Described?

There was very little information. The film was about ten years old when I and our team saw it. They just said this is the only film of the aliens and the body. There are photos taken by various citizens showing these aliens outside their craft walking around. But this is the only film that shows a close picture of the aliens and exactly what they look like. So, if you run across any more of these sightings that describe this particular 6-fingered being, you can compare against this film.

Did You Ever See The Symbols On The I-Beams In The Santilli Film?

Yes, and it was listed on documents as 'alien hieroglyphics.' Before I left the military service, I saw more information that the hieroglyphics were actually ancient Greek.
Yeah, in the reports where it mentioned alien hieroglyphics, I saw one paragraph on the last page of it that said some letters compared to early Greek. And that was in the 1950s.

The Implication Is That The 6-Fingered Humanoids Were Involved With The Inspiration Of The Greek Civilization?

Yeah, did the Greeks get their alphabet from one of these aliens? And on the craft at Area 51 closest to us, I could see some kind of hieroglyphics or writing around the outside circumference of the craft.

Were Those Symbols Indented Into, Or Raised From, The Craft's Surface?

I would say it was engraved onto the surface, just half a dozen symbols on the craft. I didn't see loose I-beams laying on the floor.

When You Saw The Drawings Of The Panels And Symbols In The Roswell File, That Was At The CIA And Not Area 51?

Right.

Do You Remember Anything More That Col. Jim Said About The Craft?

No, he kept us moving pretty rapidly. We were just supposed to get a glimpse of the craft to compare to photos submitted to us in our CIA Project Blue Book group."

What Did Col. Jim Say To Move You From The Mountain Hangar Of Discs Back To The Office Building?

He said we needed to move along to see one of the aliens in the interview room and said he wanted to have us see him. We were dumbfounded because at that moment, we had no idea we were going to be introduced to a real alien, non-human being!

Were You Expecting Then To See A 6-Fingered Being?

Yes, all of us were. Then when we saw the being that we did with the large eyes and large, smooth head expanding upward above a slit mouth and narrow chin, we were kind of shocked at how that alien actually looked. Like with the 6-fingered beings, there were muscles showing, but on the one at Area 51, he was very thin with 'anemic' arms.

From Your Close-Up View, Was The Area 51 Gray Being's Skin Textured? Some Abductees Compare Skin They Have Seen To Canvas.

Yes, the being was definitely textured and there were areas of little outcroppings on his skin that looked like a bee sting puffed up around his neck and down his arms. He wasn't completely smooth everywhere. Canvas would be a good description for it along with the anomalies on his skin.
I didn't see his lower body because he had like a T-shirt over him. I don't know why he was dressed up in human clothes.

Perhaps To Make The Being More Acceptable To Your Viewing.

I couldn't believe how big the eyes were!

So You Leave The Discs In The Hangar Inside Papoose Mountain And Walk Back Into The Office Complex Connected To The Mountain.

Telepathic Exchange

Yes and Col. Jim said we could 'talk'to the alien for maybe ten minutes. I don't know what the big rush was. It was like they needed to take the alien somewhere after we saw him. Col. Jim said the alien being does not speak to you verbally, only telepathically. That's when I talked with my boss, Jeffery Wright about my growing up being taught that demons were telepathic and I was afraid the creature in the office was a demon. So I asked Jeffery to ask the being if it was a demon and where it came from and how old it was. Jeffery said he did ask my questions.

I stayed outside about 20 feet from the one way mirror that I could see through into the office where the gray being was, but inside the office what I was looking through looked like a mirror. So, I could see the being and I could see it was not very tall, probably 5 feet or a little less, but definitely taller than three feet like the 6-fingered ones.

When my boss, Jeffery Wright, went inside the office, I could see the being sitting behind a table. And then when the pressure got to the alien after Jeffery asked if the being was a demon.

My CIA boss explained that when you came up with a question in your mind none of the humans had to say the question out loud. The gray being could read your mind and answer telepathically before you could even say the question.

Did Your Boss Explain Later What The Gray Being's Telepathic Communication To Him Sounded Like?

From the description that they gave that it sounded more electronic than a human voice; a neutral voice that didn't sound high or low. But that still reminded me of the description of demonic voices when I was a child. Jeffery first said out loud, 'Are you a demon?' And the being appeared frustrated or nervous.

Was The Being Sitting Down?

Yes, and the being moved around and communicated back to their minds that he was not a demon. Then the other CIA agents there asked the alien where he was from. The being answered, with some kind of star or galaxy area with a number that no one had ever heard about before. Then Jeffery asked the being if it was a demon possessing the alien body. 'Do you possess these gray alien bodies because demons don't have the power to manifest themselves as physical beings?

The gray being looked up at the ceiling and made some kind of sighing sound and looked upset and did not answer the question.

Jeffery asked a second time. Then the being got up and started pacing back and forth with its hands behind its back, but in front of the table. Kind of walking sideways back and forth with his hands out of sight like he didn't

Gray Being Upset by Demon Questions
Anonymous would not go into the interrogation room for fear the alien being was a demon.

want us to see his hands. And we couldnt' see the being's feet because the lower part of its body was behind the desk. Then the being sat down again.

But when Jeffery asked the first questions about the alien being a demon, Jeffery could hear the answers in his head, but the other men could not hear the answer. Only the person who was communicating with the alien would hear the answer back, not the others. So the men began repeating the questions and answers out loud.

Did Anyone Ask The Gray Being, 'Why Don't You Telepath To All Our Heads So We Can Hear Everything At The Same Time?'

Yes, they did and the being said he was communicating the way he communicated, like one-on-one. So, when they spoke out loud each other's questions, that was the only way the men knew what each was asking. And each man had to repeat the answer he individually heard in his mind from the being.

You Are Watching And You Could See The Moment Where The Gray Being Got Up And Paced. Did You Ask Jeffery Wright Later Why The Being Seemed Upset?

Yes, I did and Jeffery said he was trying to ask the question, my demon questions and was afraid if he kept on asking my questions, the being might leap across the desk and try to strangle him. "Anonymous" you really pushed this alien's buttons,' Jeffery said to me laughing.

I wondered then if the gray being was upset because it actually was occupied and operated by a demon like demons can possess human beings.

Gray Beings and 6-Fingered Beings- What is the relationship?

Why Wouldn't Jeffery Wright Have Asked The Being To Show Its Hands Since You All Had Seen The 6-Fingered Autopsy?

I think Jeffery just thought at the time all aliens had six fingers. I asked, 'is this the only alien you have?' Col. Jim did not answer that question, but said, 'if you've seen one alien you have seen them all.' Which I know now is not true.

Why Didn't You From The CIA Say You Had Seen An Autopsy Film Of A 6-Fingered Being That Didn't Look Anything Like The Gray In The Area 51 Office Complex?

We did bring that up with Col. Jim right before our CIA group went into the room with the being. Col. Jim said something like, 'this is an alien called a gray.' Some of the aliens have different features. There are different kinds, but this happens to be a 'gray.' The 6-fingered ones looked gray-colored too.

Did Jeffery Wright Ask Col. Jim If They Had A 6-Fingered Being?

I did ask Col. Jim exactly how many aliens they had there at Area51, but he would not answer the question.

Did You Persist About The Autopsy Film Of A Being That Didn't Even Look Like The Gray In The Office?

Not really because Col. Jim did say before the meeting with the alien that there were different types of aliens. Jeffery mentioned the autopsy film and Col. Jim stressed the gray alien in the office was entirely different from the being in the autopsy film.

Did Any Of You Ask What The Relationship Was Between The Different Alien Types?

Col. Jim did say they all seemed to say the same thing; that they were all here to be a help and not a hindrance, that they were not coming here to destroy the United States or the world.

Did Jeffery Wright Ask How Many Different Non-Humans Were On Earth?

Yes, he asked the gray alien that question and the alien refused to answer.

Wasn't There A Discussion Between Your Boss And Col. Jim About Why The Gray Being Was In The Office?

Jeffery asked how long the being had been there? What was our government doing with the alien? Where else was it going? Col. Jim answered that the being had been at Area 51 for some time. But he would not say how long.

How Did The Session With The Gray Being In The Office Come To An End?

Col. Jim was in there with my boss and the other guys at the beginning. But then he came back out into the room where I was and seemed to be bored by the same questions that others asked the gray being before in other sessions. He looked at his watch and went back into the office and said, 'this is the last question.'

After You Left Area 51 Did You Go Back To Your Base?

Yes, all five of us (Anonymous, Jeffery Wright and three other CIA agents.)

It's August 1958 And You've Been Exposed To The Live Non-Human Being. You've Been Exposed To The Seven Discs. You've Seen The 16 mm Filmed Dissection Of The 6-Fingered Beings. You've Been In The CIA Library And Seen Files Concerning Roswell And The Retrieval Of At Least Three Kinds Of Discs, Plus There Are German Made Discs In Argentina And Antarctica.
You Go Back To The Eastern Base And Your CIA Project Blue Book Unit. What Kind Of New Work Do You Do?

When we got back, we had quite of few UFO sighting cases. One was from Puerto Rico. Some more in France and Belgium.

What Was The Most Dramatic?

I think the Belgium one. It was a triangle-shaped craft and had lights in each of the three corners.

So All The Way Back To 1958, You Had Reports And Photos Of Triangles In Belgium Like The 1990 Reports?

Yes. But is was a fairly small craft back in 1958. I think the ones in the 1990s were very large.

What Was The Discussion Between You And Jeffery Wright And The Others In Your Unit About The Triangle Craft?

We were dumbfounded because we had never seen anything else up to that point except round discs.

Cigars?

We didn't see cigar shapes until probably 1960 when we had a cigar-shaped craft in the atmosphere flying along at 5,000 to 6,000 mph. That was the only cigar-shaped craft that we had pictures on.

Was It On 16 mm Film?

Yes.

Who Took That Film?

It was foreign and I think the craft was down in Spain coming off the Mediterranean.

The Triangles Were Only In Belgium?

The only time I saw a photograph of a triangle-shaped craft, it was in Belgium and it came in from the coast into Belgium and then went back out to the English Channel before it went to Holland.

Did You Sit Down With Jeffery And The Others And Say; 'Ok, This Is What We've Seen. Now Is This New Photo A German Craft? Is This New Photo A 6-Fingered Type? Is This Gray?'

When we first saw the triangle-shaped craft, our first thoughts were that it was a phony picture because we had not seen anything that was triangular before. In fact, for that triangle in Belgium, we didn't have much of a write-up. Langley and Ft. Belvoir never confirmed that it was an authentic photograph, not a hoaxed double exposure. So, we checked back with Ft. Belvoir to see what else they had on the triangle craft. They said, 'We checked the photo, but the grain in the photo is apparently authentic. It's not a triangle hanging on a string.'

So, It's A New Craft And Nobody Knows Who Is In It?

Right, no one told us if they knew. I believe that was the first photo that our CIA Blue Book project ever passed on to us that was triangular instead of round.

Different Aerial Craft: German and Interplanetary

Did You And Jeffery Sit Down And Talk With Each Other About Which Type Of Non-Human Was In The Triangle, The Disc, The Cigar And Various Craft Types?

Yes, we figured the different shapes came from different parts of the universe maybe and that there probably are different types of aliens in the different craft. We did try to identify some of the foreign photographs. There was one from South America that we identified as a German Haunebu II.

You Did Have A Photograph That Confirmed The Germans Were Still Flying Some Of Their Peenemunde Craft In South America?

Oh, yeah! The craft with a high center about 12-feet high, they all look like Haunebu IIs. Although they could be alien craft as well. But we labeled those photos as being German Craft from Argentina.

However, on radar, we used to see some of the real alien craft come from outer space right down into the Argentina region. We also saw craft come into the Antarctica region from outer space via radar we shared with the British down in the Falkland Islands in the South Atlantic Ocean east of Argentina. The British would send us radar tapes of UFO craft coming in at terrific speeds and down into the Antarctic region.

Do You Mean That The Radar Confirmed Something Not From Earth, But Really From Outer Space, Was Working With The Germans On Craft In Antarctica And Argentina?

Yes, that was the implication. In 1959 to 1960, our unit was separating alien craft from the known German craft by the appearance of the craft. We always found the German craft to be much slower in speed than the alien craft. Some alien craft were tracked from outer space doing something like 30,000 mph.

[Editors Note: Agent Anonymous makes reference to German U-Boats deployed to Argentina with a cargo of Nazi scientists, SS officers and other high-ranking Nazi officials. They traversed major Argentina rivers in order to reach the Nazi encampments in the interior regions of Argentina.

Other researchers have established that over 100 Nazi U-boats along with their captains, were unaccounted for after WW II by the allied powers. Researchers have suggested that part of the cargo was some of the Nazi's most secret advanced weapons systems.

There have been mutiple UFO sightings over all of the countries of South America and Antarctica for over 60 years.]

Alien Agenda: Human abductions, Animal mutilations, Implants

What Were The Discussions In Your CIA Group About What The Beings Or UFOS Wanted?

We were always trying to get more information from Langley headquarters as far as the beings were concerned. Sometimes we had a huge amount of military sightings; something that we knew were completely legitimate observations of alien activity. All of a sudden we would have dozens of alien craft in one region on Earth in military radar screens that just flew right over at huge speeds. Those we knew were authentic because they were recorded on military equipment. We also had moving film of the craft on radar because there were cameras that could film the radar screens.

Did Anyone Say, 'These Are Hostile?'

No. But I think we had a couple of civilian reports about people abducted in Greece or Italy. There was one person who disappeared while walking up to look at a craft. The person either disappeared or was taken aboard the craft, examined, and then was found laying on the ground away from the area where the craft had originally landed.

These Were 1958 To 1960 Reports Your CIA Unit Received?

Yes. We also had animal mutilation reports back then. I remember Colorado was one place. Those events were investigated locally by some agents, but not by us because our focus was international events. But we received photos and information so we would know what happened to the animal bodies to be able to look for the phenomenon in foreign sites.

Did The Reports To Your CIA Office Say That The Animal Mutilations Were Directly Linked To Extraterrestrial Craft?

Yes, because they had saucer craft spotted in the area and seen by ranchers. Then the ranchers found the mutilated animals near a saucer sighting.

When You Got Those Animal Mutilations And Human Abduction Reports, You Would Say What In Your Meetings?

Why are the aliens doing this? Why are they taking certain parts of these cattle and other animals. The reports we read said there were mutilations of other smaller animals, not just cows and horses.

Jeffery Wright came up with a twist. Our reports said that the sex organs were usually taken along with other parts and Jeffery said, 'maybe the aliens were using them becaue we had seen the autopsy of the 6-fingered ones that said the beings were neither male nor female. Maybe they are trying to use some of this material to manufacture a being that could reproduce?' That was the main gist of our animal mutilation discussion.

About the abductions, the humans were probed and examined. We had one or two that had implants. A Woman in Puerto Rico had an implant in her neck. The agent there had a doctor remove this thing from her neck and found out it was a chip of some kind. She told the investigators that the aliens had implanted something in her, but she had a miscarriage right away. It was just a tiny little fetus and investigators could not tell if there was any difference between a normal human fetus of that age or an alien fetus or hybrid fetus.

Apparently, something like that must be some of the alien experimentation. In the Puerto Rico case, we concluded that the aliens had put the implant in her neck not too far from the spinal column that would work like a homing device. The aliens would be able to find that particular woman any time and anywhere she might be.

So, You Were Dealing With Abductions, Implants, Animal Mutilations, Craft In Which Some Were Said To Be German And Some Extraterrestrial, 6-Fingered Humanoids And Gray Beings. All In That Short Period Of Time Between 1958 And 1960?

Yes. As far as the animal mutilations, our CIA Project Blue Book unit was not investigating the animal mutilations, but we were sent two cases from Colorado so we could see how the aliens were mutilating the animals.

During my time with the CIA unit, we never ran across a foreign mutilation; or at least none were sent to us.

CIA Trip to Brief Richard Nixon

Did Jeffery Wright Ever Go Back To Washington, D.C. To Ask For More Information Because The Story Was Getting To Be So Much More Complicated?

Yes, the second trip when we went there and actually got into the White House was to see Richard Nixon at that time. I think that was late 1958 or early 1959.

Soon After Going Out To Area 51?

Probably four or five months later and we went over all this material with him.

With Richard Nixon?

Yes.

In The Oval Office?

Yes. And we had other people there with us from the CIA and they said, 'We're trying to send you everything that we have.' We told them we had no foreign animal mutilations ever sent to us. But we had the Puerto Rico case of the 'tagging' of this woman. They called it 'tagging' when humans had implants in their neck or back or something like that. The other CIA people told us they had many cases of that occurring in the United States.

Tagging?

Yes. 'Tagging' was when non-humans put little chips into the necks of people. The CIA had many cases. One implant device was supposed to have produced hieroglyphs when passed over a certain kind of scanning device. That was in 1960 just before I got out. The woman with that implant had been taken up in a craft that started out above her, then shone a beam of light down on her. When she was inside the beam of light, she floated up into the craft.

Did She Remember Anything Consciously?

No but under hypnosis she said that she was put on a table and examined and that the aliens had a probe come down that implanted the chip in her neck. After that the aliens did not do anything of a sexual nature to her, but they gave her a thorough physical body exam, even her feet. She had a toe that had a problem, like a hammer toe. The aliens focused on that and ran some kind of gizmo over her big toe. She had a terrible arthritis in that toe. But after she had no more arthritis at all in the small toes. The aliens helped her and took the arthritis away.

Did She Describe The Beings?

If I remember correctly, she described them as small, about three feet tall, like grays with the big, dark eyes, and pointed chins.

The Same Type As The One At Area 51 That You Were Afraid Was A Demon? What Did You Think About This Case When You Learned The Beings Had Healed Her Toes?

Well, we knew the aliens had various technologies such as laser cutters and other advanced tools. We just thought there was some kind of tool with a bright light they ran over her toes like they were trying to straighten her toe out.

At That Point, Were You Re-Evaluating The Issue Of Demons? Did You Consider That Non-Humans Might Have A Vested Interest In Earth That Was Not Necessarily Evil?

Yes. I would say we kind of swung back and forth, all of us swung back and forth. We thought there were some good aliens and some bad aliens, just like there are good and bad angels and good and bad humans. We thought some really were helpful and didn't seem to do any harm to anybody. But why did they implant that particular woman? Maybe to see how the toes turned out. We didn't know.

What Did Richard Nixon Say?

First of all, he walked in and then we all sat down. The CIA used to always tease Nixon. The guys for some reason loved to tease him. They told him that somebody is out to kill you and he would flash his hands around. One time he called out my name and asked, 'why do you always sit there?' And I answered, 'well, this is the first time I've ever been here. I think you've got me confused with someone else. But I sat here because I have a better shot from here.'
Nixon looked at the door and said, 'That's a good idea. Good thinking.'

But I was trying to tease him like the other guys. All through his career, the CIA always hassled him about somebody being out to get him. It was our big inside joke.

What Did Nixon Know Concerning The Aliens?

He didn't have that much knowledge. He said, 'From all the reports I have received, we don't know if they are trying to survey Earth for attack later. We don't know. Some apparently do good. Some torture people and let them go. Or we are missing people altogether. We don't know if some ever came back that were abducted and we have no idea where the aliens took them or where they went.' That was the whole gist of information up to 1960 that we really were not sure whether the aliens had come to kill us eventually or come to help us or what? Why were they here on Earth? Why didn't they go someplace else and leave us alone?

You Had The Meeting With Nixon To Decide What?

In that white house meeting, we were reporting to Nixon because he helped President Eisenhowere out in foreign affairs and Nixon always wanted to know everything that was going on in the foreign nations. He was very good at that and very knowledgeable. I never liked his personality, but he had a good mind. That might be why CIA people were always teasing him, trying to lighten him up? (laughs) Nixon must have been really paranoid!

Did Nixon Ever Sit In On A Meeting With You And Jeffery Wright?

One time with President Eisenhower and Nixon. When Nixon was covering foreign issues, Eisenhower would sort of let him speak to see what comments Nixon had. One time Eisenhower got very aggravated with Nixon and told him to shut up.

Eisenhower was very hard nose military. There was no joking with him. Everythhing was absolutely cut and dried and you kind of hoped to get out of his office as soon as you could.

What Did Eisenhower Say About The Extraterrestrial Presense?

He said, 'I can't figure out why we can't get to the bottom of this!'

"To finish their meeting with Vice President Nixon the FBI had a short film about a saucer materialzing over a power station. Nixon said he brought us in to the FBI and USAF meeting to see that 16 mm film of the UFO."

-Anonymous, Former Army/CIA UFO Analyst

What do you remember that Nixon specifically said about the UFO phenomenon?

Nixon asked Jeffery Wright and me about how many foreign reports there were and if any of the CIA spies in the Soviet Union had seen any reports about contacts with aliens. We said, 'Yes, they have,' and we told them about an incident with the aliens that almost triggered a nuclear war. A saucer craft was hovering over one of the silos for their rocket launching facility in the Soviet Union and all the switches turned on after the aliens interfered with the electrical fields. The engineers tried to shut off the switches, but the switches would not shut off.

What Year?

Early 1959 probably because I think we were at the White House for the second meeting when the cherry blossoms were out in Washington, D.C. like late March or April.

Did you have three meetings in Washington,D. C.?

Yes, but the first one was cancelled.

That's When You Went To The CIA Library?

Yes.

[Editor's Note: In previous reports of long 1998 discussions with Anonymous, he referred to the Langley CIA in what had become a generic name for the agency by then. The Central Intelligence Agency was created on September 18, 1947 by President Harry S. Truman's National Security Act of 1947. The CIA replaced the National Intelligence Authority (NIA) and the Central Intelligence Group (CIG.) At first, the newly created CIA personnel moved into 2430 E. Street N.W. that had housed the OSS (Office of Strategic Services) during World War II in a low-lying region of northwest Washington, D. C., known as Foggy Bottom.
    As the CIA grew, it spread into three dozen CIA offices scattered around the nations' capitol. On August 4, 1955, President Dwight D. Eisenhower signed a bill authorizing $46 million for construction of a CIA headquarters building. On November 3, 1959, the cornerstone and time capsule were placed in the new Langley, Virginia, CIA headquarters.]

The Second Meeting Was Only With Vice President Nixon?

Yes. The third was with President Eisenhower and Nixon together in the Spring of 1959.

Let's Go To The Meeting With Nixon Without The President. When Was That?

It was cold. It had to be like November or December of 1958.

Were You With Jeffery Wright?

Yes, the two of us went together.

Were You Made To Sign Any Specific Non-Disclosure Oath In Order To Get The Top Secret White House Security Clearance?

Yes. We had to sign an oath that we would follow all the procedures and rules and regulations about handling classified material to the length of the classification, kind of a generalized oath for handling classified materials.

Did It Have Anything About Punishment If You Talked?

Yes, that you would be arrested and put on trial for passing on classified materials.

You Told Me You Thought After 35 Years Your Oath Would Be Lifted?

Yes when I started working with cryptography, that had a non-disclosure limit of 35 years related to cryptography classified materials. Also, when we started the CIA Project Blue Book study of international photographs and films or sketches, our non-disclosure agreement was for 35 years.

That Ended When?

1995.

Getting Into White House Oval Office Meeting

What Was The Process To Get Into The White House?

We flew up on Eastern Airlines from out of our military base to Washington, D.C. We were picked up there at the airport and taken to a hotel around 5 pm in Langley, Virginia.

The Next Morning What Happened?

Jeffery had called CIA headquarters regarding transportation to get to the White House. They sent one of the CIA black limosines for us. The CIA had its own cars like that for transportation for executives and people who visited to work. The limos were busy all the time.

Were The Cars Marked In Any Way?

No, there was a sticker on the windshield, which I believe did say in small print, 'CIA,' and had a code number across the bottom of the windshield. That determined for the White House guards that it was an authorized vehicle to enter the White House grounds.

What Were The Plates Like?

Government plates.

It's Fall 1958?

Yes. When they picked us up at the airport, they kept the small suitcase we had of the classified materials we wanted to show Nixon. That way, we could go to the hotel, check in with our suitcase of personal clothes and leave the classified materials in the back of the CIA limo. It was a small suitcase about twice the size of a normal briefcase that we carried classified materials in while we traveled.

What Was In The Suitcase?

Foreign photographs of alien craft that we were working on and anything that we could show as examples of the UFO phenomenon internationally.

The Photographs Were All Of Discs? Any Beings?

All discs and the one triangle from Belgium.

Was The Triangle A New Photograph Then In The Fall Of 1958?

Yes, it was probably a month old at that time.

So The Briefcase Of Materials You Are Taking To Vice President Nixon Is In The Back Of The Limousine. When You Got To The White House, What Kind Of Security Check Did You Have To Go Through?

First, the limo was stopped and the driver had to show his ID. The White House security guards also checked the ID on the limo windshield. Then we had to pull the limo ahead and roll down our windows so that security could check both of our IDs. Then the driver pulled the limo up to the side entrance and we went up to the door. There were guards there and we had to show our ID again.

Then we had to open the briefcase so they could check inside to make sure we weren't carrying a bomb into the White House, you know? That was the bomb test. (laughs)

Then we came in and walked down a long corridor and got into the Oval Office area where we waited in a small room right off the Oval Office. We told the guard there that we had an appointment and he went to check with the appointment secretary. The appointment secretary went inside the Oval Office to talk directly to Nixon. The guard took us into the Oval Office. Nixon got up from his desk and introduced us to a CIA head from the eastern U.S. in charge of using CIA field agents overseas to check Project Blue Book cases. Then he introduced USAF and FBI people. Nixon did not name them all. He named only the heads, not all of us. My boss introduced me. We went to set down and there were not enough chairs. Nixon was irritated and said he would probably have to go to Congress to get more chairs (laughs.) Then a security guard was sent for two more chairs and they brought in their two security chairs.

Why Would The FBI Have Been Involved In White House Meetings About UFOs?

Apparently because they had investigated some sightings in the local U.S. I know the local USAF interviewed eyewitnesses and asked the FBI to investigate as well.

The USAF Would Be Able To Use The FBI Because Why?

J. Edgar Hoover. This was a pet project for him.

He Was Very Interested?

Yes. At first Hoover thought it was some kind of national conspiracy produced by Soviets or South America. He was very interested from a national security point of view. Hoover was not at the meetings, but he always met with the President, Vice President and his FBI agents who were at the meetings. I think that Eisenhower and Hoover were reasonably close. Both were very outspoken men, both rough and gruff, cut you right off in the middle of a sentence. But apparently Eisenhower thought that Hoover had been very efficient over the years and did a good job.

What Was The Reason For The Meeting With Nixon?

That meeting was for a progress report about our new CIA Project Blue Book study of international UFO phenomenon incidents and aerial photographs. We reported to Nixon about the worldwide situation; what we had on UFO sightings. There were also people there in the meeting from the USAF and FBI who had all the domestic American information reports. That's the only meeting I attended in which the FBI was present with us. That morning the FBI had begun a 9 am meeting with Nixon before us. They were supposed to be done before our meeting began at 10 am, but Nixon called us in as they were finishing up.

16 mm film screened in Oval Office of UFO "Materializing" Over Power Plant

Nixon had to go somewhere the next morning (and was cramming as much discussion in before he left.) To finish their meeting with Vice President Nixon, the FBI had a short film about a saucer materialzing over a power station. Nixon said he brought us in to the FBI and USAF meeting to see that 16 mm film of the UFO.

Did Nixon Or Anyone Talk While The Film Was Screened?

No, we just watched it. There was no soundtrack, it was only silent. The USAF Colonel who was there said before it started that he was going to show an actual film of a saucer craft materializing over a power plant. Nixon said, 'Materializing?' And the USAF Colonel said, 'Well, wait until you see the film.' The Colonel said he wouldn't say more about the film because it would be self-explanatory when we saw it. The Colonel had the lights shut off and he started the projector.

In The Oval Office, Where Would They Watch A 16 mm Film?

The USAF Colonel had a portable projector that folded down into a suitcase. You opened it up and the reel arms rotated out to put film reels on. There was also a little portable screen.

Did The Air Force Colonel Set Up The Screen?

It was already set up in a back corner of the Oval Office and we had to pull some drapes shut so it was more dark in there.

Where Did Nixon Go To Watch The Film?

He sat right at his desk because he could see it from there. The rest of us had to turn our chairs around because the screen was almost directly behind us.

Did The Air Force Colonel Make Any Preparatory Remarks?

He said it was a new film and it was taken by an amateur photographer on his movie camera. He said the film was self-explanatory and we would look at the film first and then talk about it.

So he turned on the film and we watched. It was a power station. You could see the smoke stacks and steam going up and then you could see a little, white cloud that developed over the power station.

Was The Film Color?

Yes, it was a blue sky. You could see the smoke from the smokestack. Then about fifty feet to the right of that, you could see the little cloud developing and getting bigger and bigger. Pretty soon, the cloud got more round and then in the cloud itself you could see little porthole windows, as it was turning. It still looked like a cloud at that point. Then as it got bigger, the craft got more silver colored and then you could not see the cloud. The silver craft was all you could see. The bottom of the craft turned a reddish or pinkish color and then it started moving slowly away.

That was the end of the film. Nixon said, "This is a helluva thing!" Nixon swore an awful lot, almost every other word was a cuss word. He said, "I can't believe this. This saucer develops and flies away!" Then he asked if we had any information about where the craft came from. No one had any information.

Then Nixon said, 'This would be a helluva thing in a war. They could materialize over any power station and you would have saucer craft all over the Earth." Then Nixon asked, 'Do you think there were aliens in the materializing saucer craft?' The USAF and FBI guys told Nixon they had no

Nixon: "This is a helluva thing!"

idea. There was discussion about whether it was a remote-controlled craft with no beings in it. But we had no way of telling . It did look like one of the smaller alien craft at Area 51.

But None Of The Craft You Described At Area 51 Had Portholes In It, Right?

No, no portholes at Area 51. but in the White House meeting, the USAF Colonel made the comment that the craft over the power plant looked like a smaller alien craft . If that were true, then it was not exactly like the alien craft at Area 51 that my colleague and I saw. But the USAF and FBI might have had other photographs of small alien craft that had portholes.

Nixon asked us for an explanation and Jeffery said, 'we have no idea how anything does this. Perhaps the aliens have some way of taking the electrical current from the power plant and changing it into matter to be able to manifest the craft.' You could not see through the craft. It looked solid. It was not transparent. We didn't have any radar reports and there wasn't any record of radar showing it near the power plant, but it looked shiny silver and solid like a regular UFO.

I spoke up and said, 'Mr. Vice President, I think they came from far away and transported themselves here and don't have to go through the problem of going through time and space. I think they are moving point-to-point and can be here almost instantly.'

Disc and Two Non-Humans Landed Near Butte, Montana

We also went over photographs of a saucer that landed and alien beings got out at the Anaconda Copper Mine near Butte, Montana. Nixon said a saucer craft had landed near the Anaconda Copper Mine in Butte, Montana, and aliens had gotten out and someone had snapped photographs of the aliens. It looked like the aliens were picking up ore samples from the ground and taking them back into the craft. Then, the craft hovered slightly above the ground and took off rapidly. It was out of sight in only a second or two.

[Editor's Note: The Anaconda Copper Mine had a long history as one of the richest hill's on earth. As far back as the mid- 1800s Butte, Montana was a place for mining rich mineral deposits. However there was no way to transport it. When the railroad came through it lowered the costs.
A visionary miner, Marcus Daly, saw that with electricity came a greater need for copper. He purchased the Anaconda prospect and eventually built the world's largest metallurgic plant at Anaconda which was thirty miles to buried by the mining. See Wikipedia.]

Did You Recognize The Montana Craft As Anything Like The Craft You Saw At Area 51?

It was similar to alien craft we saw at Area 51, the bigger, silver craft.

Did You Have Photograph Blow-Ups For The Meeting? Or Only The Original Photos? ?

They had some blow-ups. But the photos were taken by a resident who had a cheap, small camera. And when you blow up low quality photos, the blowups aren't much help.

Color?

No, black and white.

What were you seeing in the photographs?

There were two aliens outside the craft and it looked like they were picking up something off the ground like rock or ore samples. In another photo, the beings were headed back into the craft. Another photo was the craft taking off. Another picture was real blurry like the craft had just sped away leaving streaks from the craft in the picture. With a cheap camera like that, it woudl not have any controlled shutter speed, so something that was really fast would be only a blur.

President Dwight David Eisenhower and Vice President Richard Nixon.

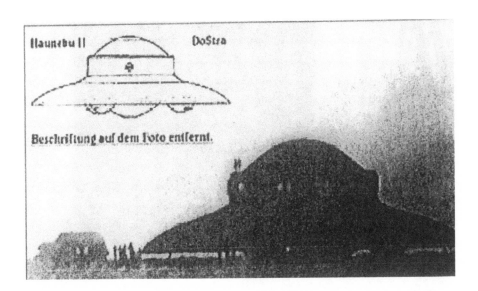

Could You See Any Details About The Alien Types?

No, it was too far away. But you could see they were wearing some kind of flight suit that was silver in color. They had something like a helmet over their heads.

How Would You Compare The Craft In The Anaconda Mine Photos To The Craft You Saw At Area 51 In Mid-August 1958?

It looked just like the biggest alien craft that we saw at Area 51 that was a silver disc.

With A Little Cupola On Top?

Yes, it had a small raised top. This one, too, had the three round nodules on the bottom of it, which looked like little radar domes.

During The Presentation Of The Photographs From Montana, Did The USAF, FBI Or Nixon Make Any Comments Aout The Beings Or Craft?

They referred to it as an alien craft. Nixon was familiar with that from seeing photographs and other briefings.

Section Four:

- Information regarding the White House Involvement in the Alien/ UFO Reality and subsequent cover-up and Intelligences agencies research
- Discussion about J. Edgar Hoover's strong interest in the UFO Phenomena
- Agents testimony about seeing 16mm film on UFO materializing over a power plant in South America.
- Discussion about Non Humans beings seen in Butte, Montana.
- More information regarding what Vice President Nixon knew about German Disks
- Agent relates that Nixon was frustrated by the Lack of Answers from Government Intelligences sources.
- The agent tells of his showing photographs to Nixon in 1958.
- Interviewee makes the point that the US Military knew of Nazi craft being photographed in Argentina.
- In addition the discussion turns to evidence that the US Navy had picked up radar evidence of UFOs coming from space and into Area 51.
- The Blind leading the Blind.
- Nixon used the term "Majestic."
- Information regarding the meeting between President Eisenhower and Alien Beings February 20, 1954.
- The FBI investigated Human Abductions and Animal Mutilations
- Further discussion about Col. Corso and Army Lt. General Arthur Trudeau

Do You Remember Anything About The Photo Comments?

The discussion was between the USAF and Nixon in regard to those particular photographs because the Air Force had investigated that particular sighting and interviewed the residents who took the photos.

What Kind Of Questions Did Nixon Have?

He asked if the people who took the photographs said anything that might help us better understand the event. The eyewitnesses told the usual story; they had seen the craft in the sky, went into their house to get the cameras, went back out and saw the craft had landed and they took photos. So time had elapsed between their seeing the disc in the sky and when they finally got their camera back outside because the craft had already landed and the alien beings were already picking up samples and going to the craft to leave.

Did Nixon Say Anything Like, 'This Looks Like The Disc We Have Photographed In Another Case?

No, he didn't. When we were in our meeting, we talked to him about the Montana disc looking like the biggest craft we saw at Area 51. Nixon told us that he recognized it, too, and thought it was the same type of craft.

Nixon Said That?

Yes.

Then Did Nixon Say Anything About The German Discs?

No. Nixon never brought that up at the meeting. All the photographs we had to show him were alien type craft, not German. At that Fall 1958 meeting with Nixon, we did not see any photographs of aerial discs that resembled any German craft. We knew the Montana craft was not a German model, but was like the craft identified as 'alien' at Area 51.

Did Nixon Have Knowledge About German Discs?

Yes, he did. We mentioned that we saw the seven discs in the Area 51 cave hangar and we recognized them as VRIL and Haunebu I and II. Nixon already knew Area 51 had some German craft.

Nixon wanted to know if anyone had found out any more information about where the aliens came from and what they were doing. The USAF and the FBI always had the same story: 'We really don't know. We think that the aliens are not hostile. We had no hostile encounters with weapons or shooting at airplanes after we lost airplanes to the aliens and their saucer craft technology in the 1940s. They gave them a complete runaround.

[Editor's Note: This is contradicted by Leonard Stringfield, long-time

UFO investigator living near Wright -Patterson AFB, Ohio, who said he was secretly told that the USAF had lost so many planes and pilots trying to shoot discs down from the 1940s to the mid-1950s that finally a shoot-down policy was rescinded.]

Nixon Frustrated by Lack of Answers About UFO Phenomena

After the USAF and FBI left the Oval Office meeting, Nixon Said, 'Boy, I guess we haven't gained a thing. Have you people learned anything more? We told him what we had but it was nothing outstanding either.

But You Had Been To Area 51 And Encountered The Craft And The Gray Being?

Oh, yes. Nixon knew we had been to Area 51.

Did He Know All About The Craft And The Being?

Yes, he knew exactly what was there. We asked Nixon if he had ever been to Area 51. He told us, 'No, but they brought me photograph of the craft and the alien'. He said he had received a complete rundown from an officer who had been to Area 51 several times and Nixon knew about the classified Blackbird project test flying and out of Area 51. So, yes he had a rundown of the whole shot about what was at Area 51.
Nixon also asked us if we had any answers from the alien about where it was from. Jeffery told him the number and really long name that was supposed to be some kind of planet. Nixon said that was the same story they had gotten from the beginning.
  We asked Nixon how long the being had been at Area 51? We wondered if it was since, the 1940s? Nixon said it wasn't in the 1940s, but that the USAF had told him the being had been at Area 51 'a good while.'
I said to Nixon, 'Do you mean that when you asked how long the alien had been there, they didn't tell you exactly?
Nixon said that the officer that brought the material to him at the White House did not know exactly how long that particular alien had been there, but thought it was a considerably long time. Nixon said he hated that when people talked to him like this! 'Considerable time' could be thirty years or six months!'

But Nixon Was Vice President Then. Couldn't He Have Asked, "When Exactly Was This Being Put In This Building?'

Right. It was like for some reason the authorities at Area 51 really did not

want to tell Nixon. I don't know why the big secret about how long that
alien had been at Area 51. It seems like the length of time should not be that
big of a thing. But they wouldn't tell us, either when Jeffery and I and the
other CIA guys were at Area 51 in August 1958.

Nixon said to us, 'when your trip to Area 51 was arranged, Ike set all this
up and OK'd all of this because you were supposed to get a thorough tour at
Area 51.' Nixon asked us how long we were there and we told him we had
only ten minutes with the alien. Then Nixon said, 'This is BS! Your Area 51
tour was supposed to be extensive.'

Then Nixon asked us, 'did you inspect the craft? If a craft like those at
Area 51 landed overseas, did you get a close-up look at them so you could
really tell if there was a match?'

We told Nixon, 'No, they just took us down the walkway and didn't let us
go beyond the ropes.'

Nixon said, 'if you want to know the truth, I think we're both on the
outside looking in on this thing and they tell us whatever they damn well
please!'

But Who Is They?

The USAF and the people running Area 51. I think it was a civilian who
actually ran Area 51.

Who?

[Editors Note: MJ-12 with the cooperation of the ET visitors are in
charge of Area 51 S-4 (Source Dr. Dan Burisch/Crain Microbiologist who
worked there during the 1990s)

I have no idea. Names were never mentioned about who was actually in
charge. We had asked who was in charge of Area 51 and the alien operation
when we were on the August 1958 tour. Col. Jim would not say anything
except, 'I'm in charge of your tour.' That Colonel gave us the minimum
information possible and we told Nixon that.

*But If The President And Vice President Had Set Up For You All. At The
CIA to Go On A Thorough Tour At Area 51 To See Aliens And An Alien Being
To Facilitate CIA Investigations Of The UFO Phenomenon Why would You
Have Not Been Taken Into Every Single Craft And Told Every Detail Known
About The Aliens?*

That's what Nixon expected. And I imagine when Nixon told President
Eisenhower, he was probably pretty upset. He got very upset whenever his

orders were not precisely acted upon. He just blew his stack. But we never heard anything more about the issue.

Then the third and last meeting in which I participated, it was with both Eisenhower and Nixon in the Spring of 1959. In that meeting, nothing was said about our trip to area 51. We only covered current UFO issues with President Eisenhower for about a half-hour."

"I wonder if this triangle craft is coming from an entirely different place? Entirely different aliens? Just what is this?"
-Richard M. Nixon, Vice President, Oval Office, Fall 1958

Did Nixon Make Any Comments About His Own Confusion Or Frustration About Who Exactly Was Running The Area 51 Operation, About Which He, As Vice President, Could Not Get Answers?

Yes, he told us he was very upset that he could not get any direct answers either. Nixon said he was passing all the information on to Ike and that it seemed like we're all on the outside looking in. Then he said being on the outside was not the place to be if you are the US President and Vice President trying to run the show. So Nixon was going to speak to President Eisenhower about that. I dont' know what happened but you would assume that Ike would have pulled whoever was in charge at Area 51 into the White House for a long talk.

Even If That Happened, Did It Change Anything?

Not that we knew. Of course, Jeffery and I never went back to Area 51 together, so I don't know if anything changed or not.

Photographs Shown to Nixon, Fall 1958

What Exactly Did You Lay Out On The Surface Of The Oval Office Desk For Nixon To See?

Different photographs such as the Italian one. We had a tape recorder with us to play back the interviews we had with the eyewitnesses. We were going to play them back to Nixon, but he said he would rather that we just tell him what was on the tape. So we talked about what was on that particular Italian tape. We had sent CIA agents to Italy to interview the man and woman, the couple.

There Was A Parallel Between The Italian Photo And The Montana Anaconda

Mine Photo—The Same Sort Of Disc And Small Beings Outside Picking Stuff Off The Ground?

Yes. The craft were not entirely identical, but they were very close and the aliens came out, picked up stuff from the ground and went back into the craft.

Italy Was Pine Cones. Montana Was The Copper Ore.

Yes.

What Other Photographs And Places Did You Show Nixon?

We had the aerial shots from Mexico. Two or three photos.

Could You See Details?

No, too far away. Too cheap a camera. I wish I could have seen the FBI photographs before those agents left the Oval Office because they had a squadron of discs in the photos. They also had fighter planes with moving picture cameras onboard that flew right up through the squadron. The squadron is the one they said looked like German discs. I imagine the quality must have been very good.
The trouble with a lot of the sightings and photographs was that people were always taking pictures with their little Brownie Kodaks.

What About Belgium?

Yes, I showed Nixon the Belgium photo (from color 16 mm film). It was a small triangular craft with lights in each of the three triangle corners.

Night Time?

It was in nighttime. You could basicly see the whole craft faintly because of light reflection on the bottom. The triangle came over a tip of France and into Belgium before it got back to the Netherlands and then to the English Channel. The triangle craft had dipped into one little Belgian towm and someone had taken a photograph at that time.

The Report Was That The Triangle Went Back Toward Great Britain?

Yes. On the report with that triangle photo, they had a radar track that followed the craft right up the English Channel and on up to the North Sea area, veered over the north of Scotland and headed for the North Pole.

Was That 16 mm Color Film? Or Still Photography?

It was color 16 mm film the eyewitness had taken, but it was at night and you could just see the lights that looked bright. The craft looked dark around the lights. You could see it was a triangular shape, but you could not see any details on the bottom.

Who Took The Film?

Someone had just borrowed a used 16mm camera and was taking film around town and was walking back to his house when he saw the craft come toward him and over the town and filmed it.

Were The Photos You Showed Nixon Blown Up From The 16 mm?

Yes, we showed Nixon blown up frames from the 16mm film, not the film itself.

What Did Nixon Say?

Nixon said he had seen a triangular ship before, too. He said it looked like a photograph that had been sent from California or Oregon that he had seen earlier that morning. So he had seen a triangular craft on a photo with the FBI and USAF before we showed him the Belgium photo blow-ups.
Nixon's only comment was, "I wonder if this triangle craft is coming from an entirely different place? Entirely different aliens? Just what is this? He was as confused as the rest of us. He didn't know what was happening.
So in Fall 1958, No One Knew.

Right, nobody, excet thee could have been people at Area 51 with much more knowledge that they weren't even reporting to the White House, you know?

Area 51- Not Honest with Pres. Eisenhower and Vice President Nixon

But There Was The Live Gray Alien At Area 51 That Could Communicate Telepathically And Apparently Had Been There For Some Time. Why Wouldn't American Leaders Be Given More Insights About Who? What? From Where?

Right, Nixon said the information he had gotten from Area 51 about the gray alien there was that they were on Earth not to do harm, but were trying to help. Nixon said the gray being gave the same answers every time it was interviewed, but nothing solid was ever confirmed. Nixon said that if the gray being got a question it didn't like, the being would not answer, just like the gray being is the top of security for someone else. (laughs)
So, Nixon was frustrated that everyone got the same information, which was basically of very little help.

Did You Or Jeffery Bring Up The Fact That You Had Asked About Whether The Gray Being Was Related To Demons In Any Way? Did You Talk About That With Nixon?

Not with Nixon, no. Nixon just looked at the beings as aliens that were able to operate on their own. The 'Extraterrestrial Biological Entity' phrase never came out in any of those meetings. Nixon and everyone else just called them 'Aliens' and that was it. No one talked about specific types of aliens. Not 'Grays,' except the only time I ever heard the word 'Grays' was when Col. Jim was taking us through Area 51 mentioned that the alien being we were seeing was a 'Gray.' That's the only time I heard that term used.

In both meetings with Nixon and the later spring meeting with Nixon and Eisenhower, nothing was discussed about the relationship between the 6-fingered humanoid and the gray beings?

No President Eisenhower just referred to them as different types of 'aliens.' At that time apparently, there was no information about the 6-fingered aliens and where they were from. At least that never came up in the meetings.

I remember saying to Jeffery after oneof the meetings, 'Gee, this was a wash! We didn't accomplish a thing!'

The Blind Leading the Blind.

Yes. I always had the feeling that whoever was in charge of Area 51 was above the normal government. The Area 51 people probably told Eisenhower and Nixon exactly what they wanted to tell them and nothing more. And as I said, even Nixon commented, 'We're on the outside looking in.'

But How Could That Have Occurred Unless President Truman Signed Some Kind Of Executive Order Setting In Motion A Group That Was Immune From Congressional Oversight? There Had To Have Been An Executive Order To Set Up The Authority Over The Alien Prenoimenon.
"Did Nixon Make Any Comments About His Own Confusion Or Frustration About Who Exactly Was Running The Area 51. Operation, About Which He,

As Vice President, Could Not Get Answers?

Well, remember that even J. Edgar Hoover took it upon himself to do whatever he thought the FBI should be doing since he invented the FBI. You could never tell Hoover exactly what the FBI should be doing because his mind was closed to outside influence.
I have a feeling that whoever was in charge of the TOP SECRET alien stuff decided what would be said or not said, including saying nothing of consequence to presidents after Truman. It seems to me that the Majestic 12 group set. up by Truman has run it all by itself outside normal channels.

Nixon Used Term "Majestic" (Military and Joint Intelligence Committee)

"Getting information out of Majestic is like milking a cow that's dry."
- Richard M. Nixon

Did You Hear Either Nixon Or Eisenhower Ever Use The Term `MJ 12 Or-Majestic 12?

[Editor's note: Majestic Twelve: Twelve military, businessmen and scientists appointed by Truman to study the UFO phenomenon in 1947]

Nixon used the term 'Majestic.' He said that Majestic started this thing and were the first people who started it in the 1940s. Nixon said,'Getting information out of Majestic is like milking a cow that's dry.'

Nixon Really Said That?

Yes.

In The Fall 1958 White House Meeting?

Yes.

But He's Vice President. Didn't You All Talk With Him About Why He And President Eisenhower Could Not Simply Order All Majestic-12 Information to Be Delivered To The American Leaders?

No.

If President Eisenhower Was Frustrated And Wanted To Get To The Bottom Of The Alien Phenomenon, Why Could't He Order Every Single Piece Of

Information That Majestic -12 Had?

Well, I know that at the last spring 1959 meeting I had with them, President Eisenhower actually said, 'We need new USAF people on this. We can't continue in the same mode we are in. We aren't accomplishing a thing. We don't know anything more than we did in the late 1940s and we need new people.'

When we walked out of the Oval Office, the USAF Colonel in that particular meeting said, 'Boy, I guess I'm fired! (laughs)

In Either The Fall 1958 Meeting With Nixon Alone, Or The Spring 1959 Meeting With Eisenhower And Nixon Together, Did Anyone Bring Up The German VRIL Cave?

No, in the spring meeting of 1959, that was the last meeting we had that I attended, We never went back. After that, Jeffery Wright was just sending reports on what he had to CIA headquarters and they in turn were taking the reports to the White House
In the spring 1959 meeting, that only lasted about twenty-five minutes, we just showed Eisenhower and Nixon aerial views that we had. We had one over Puerto Rico that I said looked like a German craft. I said to the President and Vice President. "This looks like a Haunebu II German craft."

"We (CIA) gave President Eisenhower the report we had that US naval ships had radar screen information about saucer craft coming in from outer space and going into the South Pole and down into the Argentina region."
-Anonymous former Army/CIA UFO Analyst

Talk About The Puerto Rico Photograph.

Yes. we were talking about the photograph in Puerto Rico of a flying disc. I told Pres. Eisenhower in that meeting at FBI headquarters that the photograph looked like a German Haunebu II and the President said, "I think you are right'.

Did Pres. Eisenhower Elaborate About What Was German And What Was Not In Terms Of The Discs?

No, he didn't. He just agreed with me that it looked like a German Haunebu II, so the president had to be familiar with the different types of craft, just from looking at the photographs. I always had the feeling that Pres. Eisenhower knew more than we knew and that he knew a lot more than what Nixon knew. Nixon was not completely in the loop on this material because Nixon was always frustrated that he was outside looking in.

Did Nixon Say Anything About The German Craft?

Absolutely nothing. Nixon just looked kind of blank. He looked at the photograph and at Eisenhower and me and Jeffery Wright and looked a bit stunned. So, I had a feeling that Eisenhower was keeping him outside the information loop and Nixon didn't seem to know that much about what was really going on.

You Had The Impression That Nixon Might Have Been Seeing For TheFirst Time A Photograph That Was Related By You And Eisenhower To A German-Manufactured Disc?

Yes that's the first we ever mentioned in any meeting about the German craft. At the first meeting with Nixon alone in November 1958, we didn't have any photographs of discs that looked like the German craft. The photos then all looked like the alien craft at Area 51. Nixon seemed to know that he was out of the loop and not getting the whole story. I'm sure that's what was behind his blank stare.

You Or Nixon Didn't Say Anything To Eisenhower?

No, you could never say anything like that in front of Pres. Eisenhower, like 'Why didn't you tell me?' He would kick you out of the office!

Because That Would Be Nixon Saying To Eisehhower - That He Knew He Was Out Of The Information Loop?

Yes, Nixon would never have gone to Eisenhower and asked him, 'Why didn't I get this information? At that time, Eisenhower would have chewed him up and down and never have given Nixon another ounce of information on anything. That's the way Eisenhower operated—he was a lean mean, machine! You had to carry out orders very precisely with him. One detail left out and you were in the doghouse!

1959 Argentina Photographs

After The First Meeting With Nixon Alone In November 1958, You And Jeffery Wright , Went Back To Your Eastern Military Base. What Did You Do After

*That? Did You Have Any Other Highly Classified Meetings With Anyone Who
Had Really Sensitive UFO Film Or Photographs?*

I remember in January 1959, we had a courier bring in a bunch of foreign
photographs. At that time, we had a photograph of an alien craft taken from
a United States boat off the shore of Argentina in the south Atlantic. That's
the photograph we showed Pres. Eisenhower in April 1959, and I told him
that it looked like a Haunebu II and he relied, 'Yes,' he agreed.

*The January 1959 Photographs Are The Ones You Took To The Last April
Meeting In Washington With Both President Eisenhower And Vice President
Richard Nixon?*

Yes.

*When You Originally Got The January 1959 Photos, Did You Sit Down With
Jeffery Wright To Talk About Them?*

All the photos we got at that time were aerial shots. I don't recall any of a
disc that had landed. There were eight or ten photos of craft from around
the world—Italy, more shots from Belgium from The Netherlands, from
Germany. They were all aerial shots and all, except the Argentina craft,
looked like the alien craft, not German craft. They looked like the alien craft
at Area 51. It's a possibility that Germany could have been building craft
that looked just like the alien craft., (laughs) But I don't know that.

*It Sounds Like The Majority Of The Classified Photographs And Files That
You And Jeffery Wright ; And Your Team Were Getting In The Eastern U. S.
Base Were In The Category Of Non-Human Or Extraterrestrial?*

Yes.

*Did You Ever Talk With. Jeffery Wright About Why Some Extraterrestrial
Group Would Have A Specific Technology Development Relationship With
Germany?*

No. The only reference that ever came up was that last April 1959 meeting
with the president when I mentioned that the Argentina photograph craft
looked like a German Eisenhower agreed, "Yes, I think you're right."

You And Jeffery Wright Did Not Talk About The Implications?

Yes, we did discuss the craft. We agreed that anything that looked like the three alien craft were not human made. And anything that looked like the German craft we would put in the category of German craft.

But German Craft Was The Minority Category? That Was 16mm Film Taken From The Wing Of One Of Our Planes?

I'm not certain of the millimeter on the film, but they were very good cameras because on some of the other pictures we saw were taken from the airplane, the shots were excellent. That film over the United States, we were told about it in the November 1956 meeting with Richard Nixon, but we didn't see the actual photographs in that meeting—we were given a description of the saucers in the film and another case in Montana

You Never Got To See The Film Of The Saucer Formation?

No, never got to see it because that earlier briefing group had already gone through the film and other materials with Nixon before Jeffery Wright and I joined Nixon for our part of the briefing. The only photograph that the other group had left out was the one from Montana and Jeffery Wright and I got to see it—and that one was taken by an amateur photographer and was blown up and grainy and poor quality.

Between January And April 1959 Was There Anything That Came Into Your CIA Office That Seemed To Have A Connection To The 6-Fingered Beings Or The Gray Beings Or Any Specific Alien Type?

No, at that time, as I said, all the photographs were aerial shots of saucer craft in the air.
Some fairly close to the ground, but nothing landed. No photos of aliens between January and April 1959.

Eisenhower and Nixon Meeting in April 1959 FBI Headquarters

What Precipated The Reason To Travel To Washington D.C., In April 1959, To Meet With President Eisenhower And Nixon?

By April 1959, Eisenhower was not running again for President and he wanted to get all of the different faces together of military, FBI,CIA, and so on in that spring to go over everything that they had been dong so they could finalize everything before he was out of office.

What Was The Sequence Of Events For That April 1959 Meeting?

We flew from our eastern military base to Washington, D.C. A limo picked us up and took us to a hotel. We stayed overnight. We had a morning meeting scheduled with the president and vice president. We got up early and it was a very bright, sunny day. The cherry blossoms were out, so it was beautiful driving first to the Capital building where we were to wait for other CIA officials. We weren't sure if we were going to have a meeting there in the Capitol or at the White House - or where?

We waited until a guard came to us and said he had received a call that the location of the meeting had been changed to a meeting room in the FBI building. In that last meeting, we had some FBI officials that came to the meeting involved with the project. No Air Force. Eisenhower and Nixon had already talked to the U.S. Air force the week before. So, we had to get back in the limo and go to the FBI building, not too far from the White House. We were ushered into the meeting room.

Ground Floor?

It was on about the third or second loor and Eisenhower and Nixon were already there.

What Was The Room Like? How Many People?

When we came in, the room was well lit. It was a decorated conference room in the FBI headquarters building.

Colors?

White walls. Drapes were kind of a beige and they were closed.

Was It An Amphitheater?

No, it was a flat floor and there was a long table up front. Eisenhower was there at the table along with Nixon, already sitting down. As we walked in, they were discussing some type of paperwork. The FBI people, three of them, came in right behind us.

Was Hoover There? [J. Edgar Hoover was FBI Director then.]

No, there were agents familiar with the UFO cases. And then we just sat down in some chairs and Pres. Eisenhower said, 'Oh, we were concentrating here and didn't see you come in!' He rolled his chair from Nixon and said that we needed to go over what we had very quickly. He asked the FBI if they had much material. The agents said that they had a reasonably good stack to go over. Then Ike asked us what we had and we answered about ten or a dozen cases to cover.

The President said, 'We're taking you first, so come and show us what you have.' Jeffery Wright . and I took up our suitcase and opened it on the floor and took out the big folder with everything in it and laid out the photographs for Eisenhower and Nixon, The first photo we showed was the Puerto Rico one and said to them, 'This looks like a Haunebu II German craft.

Eisenhower said, 'I think you're right.

That's when Nixon looked at Eisenhower and looked at me and just sort of looked totally stunned. I had a feeling that Eisenhower had kind of kept him out of the loop, that Nixon didn't have a lot of firsthand knowledge of these things. When I mentioned the German craft, Eisenhower did not question it so he must have known about the German space program, maybe from the time he entered office in 1952.

Did Jeffery Wright Say Anything?

He said, 'Yes, I agree that this photograph resembles the German Craft'

And Eisenhower Does Not Pick Up On Your Comments And Talk About What Is Known About The German Craft?

The only thing that Eisenhower said was that we had ships down in Puerto Rico where the photograph was taken and he also wondered if the CIA had knowledge about how many of those craft reported coming out of Argentina.

U. S. Navy Radar Picked Up UFOs
Coming from Outer Space to Argentina and South Pole

We (CIA) gave President Eisenhower the report we had that U.S. naval ships had radar screen information about saucer craft coming in from outer space and going into the South Pole and down into the Argentina region . I told President Eisenhower this from the report we had about a new package of radar contacts.

When You Said That, Did Eisenhower Have More Comments?

He did not seem surprised. He said something like, 'That is to be expected.'

Or, 'We expected this' The news didn't seem that important to him. Ike seemed like it was something Eisenhower was already familiar with and already knew and that we were just reviewing for him stuff that Ike had already seen. That's what I gathered from the meeting. He might have received a report from CIA headquarter when it first came out, but we got it in January 1959.

Or Got It From Majestic 12?

I don't know how long Majestic-12 people were in business. I do know there were references to Majestic-12 back to the 1940s. I don't know if they existed under that specific name or at the end of the 1950's.

President Eisenhower Referenced Majestic-12

Did Eisenhower Ever Reference Majestic 12?

Yes. At one time, we were looking at the different photographs and Ike mentioned that he had told Nixon. 'This looks familiar.' It was an aerial shot of The Netherlands, Eisenhower said 'Contact Majestic-12 on this and verify if this is the same thing that MJ-12 had sent three months ago,' or some time line like that.

Did Nixon Respond?

Yes, he said he would check that afternoon.

Did Anyone Explain To You Why The Word, 'Majestic'?

We knew it was the term for the original people who were digging into the flying saucer episodes. That study group was labeled Majestic-12, and they were the first people involved with the federal government's investigations in the 1940s. But I really don't think 'Majestic-12" as named existed at the the end of the 1950s.

It Might Have Changed Its Name, But It's Still Referred To As 'Majestic - 12 Today By Investigators.

[Editors Note: The term MAJIC stands for—Military And Joint Intelligence Committee]

Yes, And The Classification Term, 'MAJIC'—Top Secret, Eyes Only, MA-

JIC' Was Used By The OSS (Office Of Strategic Services In WWII) As A Cryptography Term During The World War II. I'm Assuming That `Majic' With A 'J' Was A Play Off The OSS's 'MAJIC', Both Were Highly Sensitive And Classified Categories.

I never saw anything in regard to "MAJIC ', but I heard about Majestic- 12 in CIA meetings and what they were doing. We never got any photos that were stamped on the back. 'MAJESTIC-12' , or `MAJIC, or 'MAJESTIC', or any thing like that.

Maybe There Were Parallel Tracks Of Intelligence And That Majestic-12 Might Have Been Working For The National Security Council? The CIA Would Have Been Doing Its Own Intelligence Investigations. The FBI Would Be Doing Its Own Investigations. The Army Air Force, Navy And All Those Parallel Tracks And Sometimes Investigating Each Other.

Yes.

Did Eisenhower In That Meeting Say Anything About Whether He Perceived Anything As An Ally? Or Threat? From The Non-Humans?

No. In fact, the comment Ike had told Nixon that Nixon told us was that we were not gaining enough ground on the UFO phenomenon, that we needed new blood to investigate especially in the USAF as far as what Air Force was coming up with.

Is The April 1959 Meeting When Ike Said He Did Not Understand Why Nobody Was Getting To The Bottom Of The Ufo Phenomenon?

Nixon said Ike was really disappointed in the UFO research and that we needed new blood to move it all along because no one was accomplishing much. Nixon said that was Ike's perception and that's when the USAF Colonel said to Jeffery Wright and me, 'Well, it looks like I'm out of a job!'

But Nixon Told You That After Your First Meeting With Nixon Only In November 1958.

Yes.

But In The April 1959 Meeting With Eisenhower And Nixon Together, Did Eisenhower Say Anything With Impatience, Anger Or With Any Emotion That Would Give Insight About The Alien Agendas. Gray Beings?

The only thing Ike said was. 'Do you have any photographs with aliens simi-

lar to what you had before (in November 1958 meeting with Nixon)?'
We told him no, that we did not. We had interviews with the people who
took photographs of the craft and aliens, and the photos had been verified
as accurate and not phony. I think we sat for fifteen or twenty minutes with
Pres. Eisenhower and he said, 'Are these (aerial photos) the only things you
have?' We told him yes. He looked at everything, paged through them, and
we told him that all our overseas interviews described the craft and how
long it took the craft to fly over the various areas. We had one photograph
we showed Ike that was from Holland where a craft hovered over a little
town.

Craft Shape?

That was just a round one. (There was a triangle in a Netherlands photo.)
When that round disc started moving upward, it took off at high speed and
darted away. Eisenhower said. ' Yes, that's almost a run of the mill alien saucer story.' Ike specifically said 'alien saucer' about that Holland photograph.
At that time, President Eisenhower seemed very pushed, like he had a lot on
his agenda.

Did President Eisenhower Visit An Alien Being in California on February
20, 1954?

*There Is A Rumor That President Eisenhower Went To See A Non-Human
Being In California.*

I never saw anything like that in any meeting we had and nothing was ever
brought up that Ike had seen an alien or spoken with an alien or whatever it
might have been.

[Editor's Note: On February 19, 2004, The Washingtoh Post published a
50th anniversary update by reporter Peter Carlson about President Dwight
Eisenhower's visit to Palm Springs California, on February 20, 1954. UFO
Evidence archived the Post article this way:
- Fact: Associated Press issued a bulletin that night: "Pres. Eisenhower died
tonight of a heart attack in Palm Springs." Two minutes later, the AP re-
tracted that bulletin and reported that Ike was still alive. [Pres. Eisenhower
did not die until 1969.]
- Fact: His press spokesman told reporters that Ike had visited a dentist the
previous night because he had chipped a tooth while eating a chicken wing
at dinner.
- Fact: No dental record was ever presented to the media by dentist, Francis

A. Purcell, D.D.S., who died in 1974.

- Fact February 21,1954: The next day, Pres. Eisenhower attended a Church service in Los Angeles.

- Never-Explained Fact: Why did the Associated Press release a bulletin that Pres. Eisenhower died the night of February 20, 1954?

- Speculation/Rumor: President Eisenhower met with either one or more blond-haired humanoids referred to as "Nordics" or that he met with one or more gray-skinned, large black-eyed, non-humans referred to as "Grays" in a meeting at Edwards AFB or China Lake about non-human warnings that nuclear warfare would not be allowed on Earth and that nuclear missile development must be stopped.]

FBI Was Investigating Human Abductions and Animal Mutilations by Aliens

The FBI told us that they had a lot of sightings, but nothing out of the ordinary except for human abductions. We've also had some more cattle mutilations and things of that nature, but nothing exremely different about the UFO craft themselves."

Do You Remember Anything Specific That Nixon Said Or Asked In The Meeting With Eisenhower In April 1959?

No, he said very little as we went over our material. Then he said, `Do you guys have anything else to bring up?' We said, 'No.' And he said, 'Well, we're ready for the FBI report.' Then Nixon said to an FBI representative who was there, 'In your report, is there anything that might be of interest to the CIA as far as looking for unusual types of craft overseas?' The FBI told us that they had a lot of sightings, but nothing out of the ordinary except for human abductions.

The FBI Said That?

Yes. The FBI said they were investigating two abductions in which people claimed they were taken in a saucer and came back. The two people had a neighbor who took a photograph of the craft. The two people plus the neighbor suggested to the FBI that the case was probably accurate, they told us. The FBI guy said, 'Outside of that, we've also had some more cattle mutilations and things of that nature, but nothing extremely different about the UFO craft themselves.'

Then Eisenhower and Nixon said to Jeffery and me, 'If you fellows need to go somewhere, you can go because we don't think there is much more for you to learn here in the U. S?

Did Pres. Eisenhower Ask Any Questions About Animal Mutilations And Human Abductions?

No, so he must have been very familiar with those subjects apparently.

Army Lt. Colonel Philip J. Corso Said In His 1997 Book, The Day After Roswell, That He Had Read About Unusual, Bloodless, Trackless Animal Deaths While He Was Working For The Eisenhower Administration Under The Army's Lt. General Arthur Trudeau, Appointed By Pres. Eisenhower To Be The Army's First Chief Of Research And Development Command.

Yes, when reports mentioned animal mutilations, Pres. Eisenhower and Vice Pres. Nixon did not seem surprised; like they already knew.

What Did They Know About Who, What, Why?

As I said before, I had a feeling that Eisenhower knew a lot more, and that Nixon kind of knew the basics, but not too many details.

And You And Jeffery Wright' Were Treated Only On 'A Need To Know' Basis?

Yes, and Jeffery and I both wanted to leave the meeting with the President because we kind of felt like a left foot there that day. Jeffery Wright -did not like to talk with Pres. Eisenhower anyway. He was anxious to get out of the meeting as quickly as he could. (laughs)
So, I said to the President, "Sir, we're going to be taking off for the hills of (name of state in which the eastern military base was located)"
Pres. Eisenhower said; "OK, keep us informed. Remember, if it's foreign and hot, call Richard (Nixon) because he's handling anything on the foreign affairs side. He's my right hand man on foreign affairs."
We said, "Yes we'll do that". So we turned away and were packing up our materials in our briefcases. Then Pres. Eisenhower said, "OK, guys you've got to move this thing along because I've got an 11 o'clock meeting with (J. Edgar) Hoover (head of FBI}. You know what a horse's ass Hoover is if you are late for a meeting! (Laughs) I'm the President and that doesn't mean a thing. If you're late for his meeting Hoover's going to give you hell!" (Laughs)
As we left the room, the FBI was already starting out with a photograph and Pres. Eisenhower said "Well, let's hear about the abductions first."

That's What Eisenhower Said?

Yes. "Let's hear about this abduction first and go from there."

You And Jeffery Wright Did Not Get To Hear About The Abduction Event?

No. We had heard stories, before, about abductions at the previous fall 1958 meeting with Nixon and we had materials sent to us for our general information file that showed cases of human abductions that the FBI and U.S. Air Force were handling locally in the United States.
   What Happened Next?

We walked out of the office and walked down to where our limo was parked in an executive parking lot area around the corner about a half a block away. Then it took us right back to the airport.

What Did You And Jeffery Wright Talk About In The Limo?

Well I said to him, "It felt like we were a lead balloon. we didn't float at all,' And Jeffery said, 'Well, that's true. We really didn't have much. And if we didn't get much, we don't have much."

CIA Human Abduction Case Files

"I think during the 1950s there were probably a lot more abduction cases than anyone knew."
-Anonymous, Former CIA/ Army UFO Analyst

When You Got Back To Your Military Base Were You And Jeffery Wright Able To Find Out Information About What The FBI's Abduction Cases Were All About?

We asked the CIA headquarters to give us a rundown on the particular case that was brought out in the meeting with Pres. Eisenhower and Nixon. We wanted to familiarize ourselves with what happened to the people who were abducted. But we never got any information back on the cases

In Terms Of The Discussion With Nixon Or Anybody Else In Washington, D. C. About Abductions, Do You Remember Anyone Making A Comment Or Interpretation About What The Abductions Could Mean?

We'd gotten paper work earlier about human abductions, that the abducted people reported that bright light came in their bedroom and   they floated out the windows and up into a craft and were operated on or were inspected like a physical exam. Then they were back in their beds when they woke up in the morning. I remember one example that they had was a woman who floated out her bedroom window. There was a hedge with leaves on it outside and she grabbed the hedge and let go of the leaves back through the window inside her room.

In the morning, she couldn't remember what happened. But when she saw the hedge leaves by the window, then she remembered that she grabbed the leaves and reached back toward the window sill and purposefully dropped leaves inside her bedroom and there were hedge leaves inside her bedroom. So, she knew that she definitely was abducted. She was not dreaming it.

This Is Part Of One Of The Files That You And Your CIA Unit At The Eastern Military Base Received?

Yes, it was one file we received as an example. I don't know the date of that case. I think we got that example along with other files right after the August 1958 trip to Area 51. A bunch of material was sent to us like that for our information to read in case we ran across foreign abductions.

Were You Ever In Any Discussion With Anyone About What The Reason Was For Human Abductions By Extraterrestrials?

We discussed that with our entire group down there as to what in the world the aliens could be looking for? What were they doing? At that time in the 1950's the abduction thing probably not a lot of humans were abducted then, but there was nothing really public about the phenomena. I think a lot of the abductees ten or twenty years later still had these dreams and had hypnosis and found out that they really were abducted. I think during the 1950s there were probably a lot more abduction cases than anyone knew?"

Section Five

Items covered:
- More discussion about cattle mutilations, in the US & Argentina
- Further revelations about what the CIA knew about the Nazi's move to Argentina
- Nazi's secret submarine base in Argentina
- CIA arranged for Anonymous' "Death"
- Security group, Wackenhut's involvement
- More discussion regarding Cong. Steven Schiff's (R) request to GAO about the Roswell File
- Secretary of Defense James Forrsetall - What did he Know?
- A Lot of OSS people were rolled into the CIA

Argentina Mutilation Report to Anonymous'-CIA/UFO -Unit, June-1959
In June 1959, we had received several photographs from overseas, including aerial shots, and we had one cattle mutilation from Argentina reported by the Argentinian government. That was unusual because that was the first government paperwork we had received from Argentina's version of their FBI. For some reason, that Argentina unit sent a report to the CIA headquarters in Washington, D. C., about a cattle mutilation and asked for more information from us.

Do You Remember Any Of The Details And If There Were Photographs?

Headquarters sent the file to us, but the only photograph was not very good. You would think the Argentina investigators would have done good close-ups, but the steer was only photographed in a wide shot with the abdomen facing the camera. You could see that the cow's tongue and eyes were out. The stomach, or udder, was removed. There was no walk around the animal to see different angles. There were no good close-up photographs of the excisions.

What Response Did Your CIA Team Give Argentina?

We sent a person to Argentina who spoke Spanish. He called ahead of time

and talked with the Argentina authorities. Our guy told Argentina what kind of information we were looking for and he was told by the Argentina office that the report sent to the CIA was not the first animal mutilation Argentina had. There were others, but the authorities there wanted to know what information the American CIA had on the animal mutilations.
We told them that as far as American animal mutilations, we would have to turn the inquiry over to the U.S. Air Force and FBI as far as gathering information. We told Argentina we would do that and we sent the USAF and FBI a copy of the Argentina file with the statement that our CIA office would get back to the Argentina authorities after we learned more about how many American animal mutilations had been reported. We sent the Argentina file to the USAF and to the CIA - Project Blue Book - in Washington D.C. We said that Argentina wanted more information because Argentina had several animal mutilitations over some period of time and wanted to find out more about the phenomenon.

1959 Aerial Photos of Submarines On Argentina's Parana River
At that time in June 1959, I did see aerial shots of Argentina and there were several submarines right along the main north to south river from Paraguay into Argentina. And the submarine location was north up the river, still in Argentina.

[Editor's Note: Paraguay River and Parana River join together in Parana River inArgentina. Wikipedia reports; "The Parana River in south central South America runs through Brazil, Paraguay and Argentina over a course of some 1,600 miles (2,570 kilometers.) This length increases to 2,484 miles if the distance is counted from the headwaters of the Paranaiba River in Brazil. The Parana River is considered second in size only to the Amazon River amongh South American rivers. The name Parana comes from the Tupi language and means 'as big as the sea.' "

 On the aerial photos, we could see submarine pens and there were big hanger-type buildings. It was a big complex.

Our American Satellite Photos?

I think it was a U-2 photo at that time in June 1959.

You could actually see Submarines in the Aerial Photographs?

Yes, I think it was four or five submarines, submarine pens and empty pens also. There were good-sized hangar and complex buildings and smaller of fice buildings.

Wouldn't The CIA Have Had Field Agents On The Ground In Argentina Working To Identify The Complex?

We always had field agents investigating, but whatever was behind that Argentina installation had to have severe security measures around it to pick up anyone trying to approach from land, water or air. The only photographs we ever received were from high up, such as the U-2 and from a boat on the river. We never landed there because it was heavily guarded by people in Argentina uniforms, but we assumed the installation was Nazi controlled.

Were Submarines On Argentina River Under Nazi Control?

In 1959 As Far As The American CIA And Other Intelligence Agencies Were Concerned, The German Nazi Contingency Was Still Present And Viable In Argentina With Submarines?

Yes but the submarines did not have Nazi symbols on them-only serial numbers. However, we knew they were definitely identified as German-type submarines from the end of WWII.

Was There Ever Any Intelligence Discussion About What The Strategy Should Be Concerning German Nazi Technology?

When we tried to get more information about the Argentina submarine complex, we were always shot down. The CIA wanted to keep flying U-2s over there, but we always were told by CIA headquarters that we couldn't get the OK to do anything in Argentina. We assumed it was part of the secret agreement that Jeffery Wright and I found in the basement library at CIA headquartrs in Washington, D.C. that essentially Argentina was off limits. That's why w only had a few U-2 aerials and a few river shots taken by people who were CIA but we always heard that the CIA headquarters said to our Blue Book superiors. "Don't send anyone into Argentina."

[Editor's Note: Se Peter Lavenda's book "Unholy Alliance" regarding NAZI encampments.]

This is why we were so shocked when we received the cattle mutilation photograph and file from Argentina and a disc photograph taken in Argentina, similar to the disc over Pureto Rico that we showed Eisenhower and Nixon. Remember that Eisenhower knew about the Hitler/Nazi disc craft and we operated with the understanding that it was still Hitler's Nazi sau cers and game in Argentina, no matter where Hitler was, dead or alive. Also there was a big German population that moved to Argentina in the 1920s and 1030s and to Chile and other areas in South America.

After JFK was Elected President

In the Transition from Eisenhower to Kennedy, did anything special occur in your CIA Group?

After Kennedy got in, we still kept getting UFO related material in the same manner, but we had no more direct contact with the White House after our joint meeting withEisenhower and Nixon.

Why not?

We were told to call Nixon on any important photographs or anything else outstanding and nothng more really was. In that last year of 1959-1960 Eisenhower was leaving the White House. Jeffery Wright and our group didn't have any specific contact in the Kennedy Administration so we reported only to CIA headquarters.

CIA Arranged Anonymous "Death"

After Kennedy Became President, How Did You Get Out Of The CIA Unit?

Jeffery asked me in May 1960 what my plans were, was I going to re-enlist in the Army? I told him that I was not, that I wanted out. By that time, we had so many rotten apples in the CIA — so many double agents — that I did not want to be part of `shooting pigs in a poke,' I told him. You never knew who was going to try to wipe you out next. So, I wanted out. Jeffery said, 'I can't blame you for that. If I could get out, I would.' I asked him, 'Why can't you get out?'

He told me, 'I could resign. I've been in there (CIA) long enough to retire, but I don't want to retire,' he said until a certain date — I think he said 1964 or 1965. 'I want to work that length of time and then get out.'

But, Jeffery Wright never did get out of the CIA. He died of a heart attack.

Did He Explain Why He Couldn't Get Out In 1960?

He just said, 'Once you've been in this (CIA) too long — like I've been in this for so long ¬if you get out and you have all this information, your chances are slim. Do you know what I am talking about" (implying his life woud be terminated under orders.)

I said, Yes, I can see that. I haven't been in very long at all, but I think if I stayed in my chances of surviving would be less than slim!"

Jeffery said "I've always had a plan and never used it. But we have a plan we can use when you get out. We're going to handle it in such a way that you are officially dead."

He said, "In July, in order to let you survuve gettin gout of the Army and CIA, we're gong to find a derelict who has died of dehydration in the streets. We're going to get one of the unidentified corpses tha the local police department has and we're going to put your CIA I.D. on the unidentified corpse and then cremate the body. We'll also create a will to establish your request for cremation and yoru request to have your ashes spread in the (city's nearby river.)

I said, 'That sounds like a good idea.'

Jeffery said, 'We'll do this a few days or a week after you're out of our CIA unit-that's when you'll be 'dead.'

I told him, 'Well, I might be really dead anyway!' And we laughed, but he told me, 'No, I dont' think so. When I got out on July 1960, Jeffery Wright did exactly his plan to have me 'die.' In fact, the police department had picked up an unidentified corpse and the policeman called Jeffery to let him know. Then Jeffery called a certain person in the police department to arrange placing all my identification, except my photo badge, on the corpse. What they put on the body was my social security card and a few other identifiers.

The police department's inside plant then made a report about finding my identification inside the lining of the dead man's coat, along with the CIA prepared phony will that said I wanted to be cremated and my ashes thrown into the nearby river.

That body was cremated, the ashes were thrown into the river and an official death certificate with my CIA phony name was prepared along with my phony CIA social security number.

Did You Receive A Copy Of Your 'Death Certificate?'

No.

I Wondered If Jeffery Wright Sent It To You? What Happened?

I tried to get my own records with my real name to see if they had a file or DD-214 on my phony CIA name.

Did You Contact St. Louis?

Yes, I did, and was told my records were lost in the 1973 fire. One time later, I decided to check on my phony CIA name in terms of death certificates. That was much later on when I was trying to get into the VA hospital for surgery. I asked a clerk who was there if he could check a service number of a friend of mine in the service-that I had lost contact with him. I wondered if the VA could find an address for me. The hospital clerk said, 'I'm not supposed to do this, but I'll try to pull a file on the com puter.' He *punched up my old fake CIA social security number and name and said, 'I'm sorry to tell you this, but he died August 3, 1960.'*

I told the clerk I appreciated knowing that and I further checked another way and found out that my CIA cover name was 'officially dead." (Anonymous went into private business and moved up north in the United States.)

Of the 24 people who were in that CIA unit, my boss died of natural causes and I got out but was the only one who survived out of that group. The others never made it out because they started getting involved with spying in Russian and Turkey and they were all killed.

I managed to get out through the help of my boss, but my wife never knew anything about this until about one year ago (in 1997). Everything we worked on was classified for thirty or thirty-five years. So, by the mid 1990's the classifying was over and you have a lot of people now coming out, like that military officer who wrote the book (Army Lt. Col Phillip J. Corso's) The Day After Roswell 1997) Some are talking now because they feel they can do so. (safely,"

[Editor's Note: Wikipedia - "The National Personnel Records Center, St. Louis, Missouri (NPRC-MPR) is the repository of millions of military personnel, health, and medical records of discharged and deceased veterans of all services during the 20th century. (Records prior to WWI are in Washington, D. C.) NPRC (MPR) also stores medical treatment records of retirees from all services, as well as records for dependent and other persons treated at naval medical facilities. Information from the records is made available upon written request (with signature and date) to the extent allowed by law.

On July 12, 1973, a disastrous fire at the National Personnel Records Center (St. Louis, MO.) destroyed approximately 16-18 million Official Military Personnel Files. No duplicate copies of the records that were destroyed in the fire were maintained, nor was a microfilm copy ever produced. There were no indexes created prior to the fire.

In addition, millions of documents had been lent to the Department of Veterans Affairs before the fire
occurred. Therefore, a complete listing of the records that were lost is not available.)

This photograph shows firefighters with high ladders pouring water out on the sixth floor of the Military Personnel Records Center in St. Louis. on July12, 1973. There were thousands of records stored in cardboard boxes. The fire burned for two days before firefighters could put it out.

Intimidation of "Anonymous" After I Contacted Him in May 1998

Could You Explain The Sequence Of Intimidation You Have Received Since I Called You In May 1998?

Episode 1

I got a call in early May 1998, in regard to my phone number you had from a relative. You asked me if you could interview me for radio. I said I would have to give it some thought, whether I wanted to be on the radio or not.

A month later, you called me again on May 30, 1998. At the time, I told you I would give you permission to interview me for radio (on May 31 to June 1, 1998, as long as my real name and location were not given and that you could not talk about three areas I was warned about in an anonymous phone call.

I Said 'What Do You Mean?'

When I Called You On May 30, 1998, I Was Surprised To Hear You Tell Me, 'I Think Your Phone Is Tapped.'

Yeah, I was trying to figure out how'to get in touch with you to tell you your phone is tapped without letting the tappers know!

I told you that I received a phone call from a male individual who did not say who he was and did not identify himself from where he was calling and said to me that I had talked to someone in Pennsylvania in regard to some previously classified materials. The caller told me there were several things that he hoped I would not elaborate about. Those specifics were:

1 The name of the military base in the eastern United States.

2.The hit squad that worked for the CIA and was stationed at that base.

3.The routing of spy planes from that base to Cuba and back through Texas.

The anonymous caller said that discussion of those three issues publicly could cause considerable problems for...(CIA?) because reporters might try to reach the military base to dig into files and this could be a major problem.

You Told Me Back In May That The Caller Said Those People 'Might Come

To Harm?

Yes, anyone who tried to enter classified areas could be harmed physically.

Did You Ask The Caller, 'Who Are You?'

Yes, and he didn't answer me, but he asked me if I would repeat to him what information `they' did not want on the air. Then I repeated the three issues and said, 'I can't really see the justification about most of this because it's all so old.'

He said, 'There are reasons for why these three particular issues are sensitive and I can't tell you. We would appreciate it if you don't talk about those three things.' And then he hung up.

Phone Company Executive Confirms Caller Was from Wackenhut

I had a friend who has worked years for the phone company who found out that the call to me had come from the East Coast of Florida, from the Coral Gables area. The call was made from the Wackenhut Corporation in Coral Gables.

[Editor's Note: Wikipedia — "The Wackenhut Corporation is a private security and investigation firm based in the United States with other headquarters in Europe and other international locations. Wackenhut was founded in 1954, in Coral Gables, Florida, by George Wackenhut and three partners, all former FBI agents. Wackenhut is now headquartered in Palm Beach Gardens, Florida.

In 2002, the company was purchased for $570 million by Danish corporation Group 4 Faick, now known as Group 4 Securicor. G4S ple (formerly Group 4 Securicor) is the world's largest security services provider. Its services include manned security, operation of criminal justice systems, electronic security systems and financial services including cash transfer. It is listed on the London Stock Exchange and is a constituent of the FTSE 100 Index. At the time of this purchase, the Wackenhut Corporation operated in 54 countries. Had $2.8 billion in revenue, and its founder had control over more that 50% of its stock.

The company has supplied complete police services at the Tampa Airport and pre departure security at several other airports, plus security for courthouses in Texas and Florida, armed patrols for the Miami Downtown Development Authority; guards to ride the Miami Metro Rail and the

Tri-Rail from West Palm Beach to Dade County and other assignments. In addition to security, the company also provides fire and rescue services for some clients, including the Kennedy Space Center]

Then, when you did do the radio interview broadcast of me on May 31 and June 1, 1998, you did comply and blanked out all the specific information I had previously given you about the three issues the Wackenhut caller warned me about. That way, you and I were letting them know that we were following their instructions, but getting the rest of the story out to the public.

The Caller Never Requested That You Not Discuss The Alien Beings And Craft?

Nothing along those lines, just the three issues. May I give you my guess about why I think those three issues were still so sensitive in 1998? My guess would be because of the U-2 flights that originated in the eastern state, which was TOP SECRET. That was from the very classified area, the little airport within the military base.
Further, my guess would be that Wackenhut Corp. has a man working out of that classified eastern military base as far as the black trucks, helicopters and retrievals of alien craft that might come down. In other words, Wackenhut is working with a TOP SECRET government operation to retrieve alien technologies and entities.
Also, a friend of mine who was flying over within ten miles of our secret U-2 base back in the late 1950s, he was just looking over in that direction at a plane taking off. Then he saw flashes of light coming up tremendously fast into the air right from that area, so he wondered if there might be a Star Wars-type ground-to-satellite experimentation with a goal to shoot down satellites from the eastern base. By 1998, that would still be highly classified. The airfield there is not known to most people and is well-hidden without access roads,

Anonymous's Effort to Get Paper Copy of Wackenhut Caller's Phone Number

In That Second Phone Call To You On May 30, 1998, I Said To You, 'You Need To Try To Get The Wackenhut Source Of The Phone Call On Paper In A Paper Trail With The Phone Company.' What Happened?

Right. My long-time friend at the phone company got into the computer to print out a paper trail for me of the anonymous caller's number he had confirmed as Wackenhut, Coral Gables. But because my friend was not supposed to be in that particular computer area, he sneaked in again to retrieve the phone number of the Wackenhut person who tailed me. -To my friend's astonishment, the phone number no longer showed in the phone company computer list.

He called me back to tell me and I asked him if there was any way he could find other records that would show where the phone number originated on the East Coast. My friend had called someone who worked in his boss's office and the boss's office person said she would see what the East Coast operator might find. They did check and found nothing on that end. She said, 'When this phone number was erased — which is most likely what happened — it would have been done by someone working right in the top echelon offices of the phone company, which is Sprint down here.' No one else from an outside computer could get in to erase a phone number specifically because there are security systems that are regularly changed for protection.

So The Wackenhut Selective Change Would Have To Have Been Done By A Manager In The Sprint Executive Offices In Florida?

I would imagine it was handled out of Ft. Lauderdale, which is a larger town.

Not Coral Gables?

Maybe not. And knowing that all this was being done by Wackenhut and probably the CIA, you can conclude that Wackenhut and the CIA have what you can call 'paid infiltrators' on payroll inside phone companies. So, when emergency issues like this come along, the infiltrator that monitors would call whatever its headquarters and in a few minutes, whatever the issue is, it is taken care of. In my case, it was the anonymous phone caller.

I Didn't Ask You To Get A Paper Copy Of The Wackenhut Phone Number Until Monday, June 1, 1998. That Means Someone Was Listening To Our Phone Call On May, 30th In Order-For-The Number To Disappear.

Yes, in our phone conversation on May 30, I mentioned to you that my phone company friend confirmed it was a Wackenhut phone number from Coral Gables, Florida. Assuming yours? Mine? Both of our phones were tapped and someone tapping called right down to company headquarters. It's possible some 'insider executive' working for Wackenhut/CIA went in at night and erased the phone number.

The Fact That Can Happen, What Does It Say About The United States?

Wackenhut is a company that has been covering up a lot of classified things for years.

Did You Know About Wackenhut Corp. Back In The Late 1950S?

Yes, I did. If we had some individuals that were coming in to our eastern military base- because sometimes we had civilians that would sometimes visit, not in our classified files, but to do general work. We could call Wackenhut for background checks on civilians coming to do work. Wackenhut is a worldwide security firm wiith offices in Europe.

The Final Threat Against Stein

On September 2, 1998, Anonymous called me deeply troubled, his voice trembling. I did not have phone recording equipment on at that time. He told me that morning he had gone to a scheduled doctor's appointment about his diabetes. The doctor's office was at the top of a short flight of stairs. As Anonymous reached the first step, he saw the same two men he had encountered at the shopping plaza standing at the top of the stairs. When he reached them, their demeanor was more serious than the first July 5, 1998, supermarket encounter. Anonymous told me they had another warning: "We are here to remind you again that we expect you to be a loyal American and that you will not communicate anymore with Linda Moulton Howe if you want to see your son marry his girlfriend and give you grandchildren." At that point, Anonymous' voice broke and he said, "Linda they must be tapping my house some how because no one but my son, his mother and I know he was at our place two nights ago and told us he was going to ask his girlfriend to marry him. Even she does not know yet!" I asked Anonymous if I could call him back to at least talk about the situation on my phone recording system. He agreed. September 2, 1998, Recorded Phone Discussion after Final Threat

The CIA would probably like to get rid of me, if they could find an excuse.

But It's Not Fair And It's Not Legal.

Well most of the stuff they do is not legal) Laughs) Over the years, legality was not even a thought if they wanted to do something. We all had to sign non-disclosure agreements that applied for 35 years, which in my case was up in the early 1990's. That's the only non-disclosure agreement I ever signed.

And, of course, Jeffery Wright probably destroyed all that stuff based on the comments that the men in the supermarket made that they can't find any record at all of Jeffery and what went on about CIA extraterrestrial UFO matters in the United Sates and overseas and our secret unit at the eastern military base. I have the feeling that Jeffery Wright destroyed everything! I think that's why they really can't come up with the actual names we used as cover in our CIA Project Blue Book unit, except probably Jeffery Wright's name. Those men seemed to know more about Jeffery's past, like his being in OSS.

If Wackenhut Has Been Recording Your And My Telephone Conversations From The Beginning. You Mentioned Jeffery Wright Specifically At The Start.

That's right.

I Did Not Use His Name In The Radio Broadcast.

Right, you didn't.

This Really Bothers Me That Those Men Would Be Threatening You

Yes, and I wonder if the men threatening me had access to the German Nazi file about WW II discs that Jeffery Wright and I read in the basement archive at the CIA? Or have all those files Jeffery and I saw back in the late 1950s 'disappeared?' Remember when New Mexico Congressman Steve Schiff was trying to get Roswell Army Air Field files (1941 to 1948) and was told all the 1947 air base files had been 'destroyed without authority'?

[Editor's Note: In 1993, New Mexico Congressman Steve Schiff asked the Government Accounting Office (GAO) to determine if the U.S. Air Force, or any other U.S. government agency, possessed information on the alleged crash and recovery of an extraterrestrial vehicle and its alien occupants near Roswell, New Mexico in July 1947.

Schiff told reporters: 'The GAO report states that the outgoing messages from Roswell Army Air Field (RAAF) for this period of time were destroyed without proper authority.' Schiff pointed out that these messages would have shown how military officials in Roswell were explaining to their superiors exactly what happened.

Congressman Schiff said: 'It is my understanding that these outgoing messages were permanent records, which should never have been destroyed. The GAO could not identify who destroyed the messages, or why.' Schiff said the GAO thought the messages were destroyed over forty years ago, making further inquiry about their destruction impractical.

Schiff added, 'At least this effort caused the Air Force to acknowledge that the crashed vehicle was no weather balloon. That explanation never fit the fact of high military security used at the time.'"]

Congressman Steve Schiff (R) Albuquerque, NM died March 25, 1998, at age 51 from skin cancer.

Editor's Note:

In 1993, Congressman Steve Schiff asked the Government Accounting Office (GAO) to determine if the US Air Force, or any other US government agency, possessed information on the alleged crash and recovery of an extraterrestrial vehicle and its alien occupants near Roswell, New Mexico in July 1947.

TThe file about Roswell crashes I found was down in the CIA basement archives when I was there with Jeffery Wright . That was not filed under a Roswell heading. I wonder if there was a purposefully misleading "file system" created to mislead every one. In other words, was there some classified code to really top secret files that were deliberately mislabeled to keep people, even CIA agents, from finding the real files?

They might have yet another decoy, cover name left behind by Jeffery Wright that wasn't even the phony CIA name I had and not my real name! (laughs) However, they showed me a photograph of myself from those Army/CIA days. I usually didn't get dressed up but there I was in the photograph with a dark tie and white shirt. It was definitely me, so they must have gone through all the photographs they could find from 1956 to 1960. Naturally, I was much skinnier back then than I am now. My boss, Jeffery Wright was standing beside me in another photograph the men showed me.

Those Men Did Not Say, To You, 'We Don't Want The German File To Be Discussed Because ?

No, they didn't. They just said, 'We know that you read that WWII file and we need to keep this material from the public, along with everything else I had done and seen, that I should drop everything. Now they are threatening me about my son's safety again and I think I should lay low for some period of time now. They must have someone watching me part of the time, or all of the time. They might even think I'm the person who hid in the files some of the saucer-related materials they can't even find themselves now.

They Have No Right To Do This Intimidation.

(laughs) No, they don't! But I know for a fact that several people associated with the Roswell, New Mexico, crashes in the late 1940s were terminated, killed, according to the file I read, to keep it all quiet. There was a nurse that was in the local hospital or clinic where they brought a live alien-I know later they killed her. All the public heard about was that she eventually disappeared. But the truth is she was killed by government agents to keep her from talking.

"I do remember reading a CIA file on Harry Truman in
which he was talking about the Cold War starting with
that there were aliens from outer space and some looked
like little humans and some looked like insects."
-Anonymous, Former Army/CIA UFO Analyst

**First Secretary of Defense James V. Forrestal from September 17, 1947,
to March 28, 1949, with US President Harry S. Truman
photo undated.**

[Editors Note: In 1949 Admiral Byrd's superior Admiral James Forrestal
was sent to Bethesda Naval Hospital to recover from an alleged nervous
breakdown-He ranted to the hospital saff about the Antarctic UFOs and the
underground Nazi bases. Forrestal was denied all visitors and supposedly
commited suicide after strange circumstance in his hospital room.]

Secretary of Defense James Forrestal -What Did He Know?

Was There Any Document You Saw Anywhere That Talked Specifically About The Sickness And Death Of Secretary Of Defense Forrestal?
Yes. When I was going through the CIA files, Jeffery Wright told me that government agents had killed Forrestal.
Who Specifically Did The Killing?
It had to be the CIA. We were leaving the CIA archive and on the way out, Jeffery said, `They killed Forrestal.' And I said, 'They killed Forrestal? I thought he was killed in an accident.' Jeffery said, 'No, they killed Forrestal.'

[Editor's Note: Wikipedia - "Forrestal's sudden death on May 22, 1949, resulted from a fall out of a Bethesda Naval Hospital window. An official U.S. Navy Medical Review Board convened on his death, after examining all doctors and witnesses who were in the vicinity, could not establish the reason for Forrestal's fall (i.e. suicide, homicide, accident). Although an autopsy was performed, the autopsy report has never been made public. The peculiar circumstances of Forrestal's death, and the U.S. government's withholding of the complete report of the review board until 2004 has led to much speculation and controversy."In his book, UFOs and the National Security State: An Unclassified History, Volume One, 1941 to 1973, © 2000 by Keyhole Publishing. author Richard M.-Dolan wrote about Forrestal's mysterious death:
"At around 2 a.m. on the morning of May 22, 1949, America's first Secretary of Defense, James Vincent Forrestal, fell to his death from a small window of the 16th floor of the Bethesda Naval Hospital."
The decline and death of Forrestal is an unresolved problem of history. There is no question that he suffered from a spectacular mental breakdown during 1948 and 1949. Exactly why he did so is less certain, but the answer may have relevance to American national security — and the pesky topic of UFOs.]

Did Forrestal Know About the Non-Human Situation?
Probably

Why Has The CIA Killed People To Keep The E.T. Situation Covered Up?

I'm not exactly sure. I do remember reading a CIA file on Harry Truman in which he was talking about the Cold War starting and that there were Aliens from outer space and some looked like little humans and some looked like insects.

Who Had Written That?

I don't remember. It had to be someone who had taken down his comments in a meeting.

Truman Formed The CIA.

Yes, I Know He Did In September 1947.

Is It Fair To Say That The People Picked For The New Central Intelligence Agency In 1947 Would Have Been From The Same OSS Intgelligence Crowd That Worked On Cracking The Japaneese Code In WWII?

Any Photographs Or Drawings In The File?

No it was printed out like the minutes of the meeting.
I know a lot of people from the OSS were rolled into the CIA:

Just Like .Jeffery Wright,

Yes, he was just rolled right over into it from the OSS.

So, In The Truman File You Saw In The CIA Basement Archive, There Was A Memo About A Meeting Of The New CIA And President Truman?

Yes, the document quoted Truman saying something like,'We've got the Cold War situation. These Russians are going nuts. We have enough to deal with on that front and now we've got aliens that look like little humans and others that look like insects.'

Was There. Anything About What Forrestal Might Have Done Or. Said That Would Merit His Assassination By The CIA?

There was nothing in the file that explained why because after Jeffery told me the CIA killed Forrestal, I asked him why they would do that. And he said he did not know, but that maybe Forrestal - as the new and first American Secretary of Defense — thought the government should be honest with the public and tell about the alien retrievals."

That Was The Last Conversation I Ever Had With Anonymous Because He Asked Me Not To Phone Or Write Him Any More.

Post Script Summation

[Editor's Note: In preparation for this book I have had many opportunities to talk with Anonymous about the content of the transcripts over a period of fifteen years. The following is a summary of what we feel are the most important facts to stem from this disclosure.

There are many claims to be found on the internet or in books and there are equal amounts of debunkers who will endeavor to shake the reader's confidence in the veracity of these claims. Everything in this book is shared with you from the direct experience of a man who has had to live in the shadows because he spent his younger years in the service of our country. Due to his intellectual ability he was asked to differentiate between hoaxes and true encounters with alien beings. He saw with his own eyes the existence of alien craft and saw an extraterrestrial being. Whether or not you believe him is your choice. He was sworn to secrecy and put his life at risk to share what he knew to be the Truth. Anonymous is a deeply religious man. He had to face his own fears about how there could be civilizations other than the human beings he believed were the only occupants of the earth. Anonymous is in poor health. He made the commitment to see that this information is shared before he leaves the earth to be with his maker. It has been a burden weighing on his shoulders since his days in the CIA in the late 1950s to early 1960s. This is a long time to be carrying a secret that changes the very course of human history. It changes everything we are led to believe about our Government, our world and our nature as human beings. Anonymous is not revealing his name until after his passing to protect his family, but he essentially lost his identity when his CIA boss faked his demise so he could leave the service. The following is the essential facts that Anonymous believes are integral to an understanding of what the truth is about UFOs, Secret Government and what you do not know about Alien Encounters. Do with it what you will. But at minimum open your eyes to the many possibilities that are your right to know.]

Points that Anonymous has made which are not in the established UFO — ET literature

1.His detailed briefings in which he establishes without a doubt that he and his boss of the CIA Headquarters in the:.eastern quadrant of the U.S. gave briefings to both President Dwight D. Eisenhower and Vice President Richard M. Nixon on at least six occasions during the 1957 to 1960 time frame, in the Oval Office.
2.That the FBI was very much involved in briefing the Eisenhower administration on UFO matters.
3.Very revealing is his testimony regarding how close to the vest the CIA hierarchy kept the information secret even from their own agents until the very last moment. (example when Jeffery Wright received the Autopsy film — He didn't know what was in the canister until he put the 16 mm film in the projector...
4.Anonymous' harrowing escape from the clutches of the CIA silence enforcers.
5.The most startling information conveyed, to the Stargate Production staff, is Anonymous' explanation, in the camouflaged CIA files in the Langley archive section. about Hitler's escape to Antarctica and South America after WW II. When history investigators dig into this part of Anonymous' testimony it will rock the world. All of the History Books will have to be rewritten

Epilogue of Anonymous interview:

Anonymous confirms suppression of information that the US Navy met with hostile forces in Operation High Jump at the end of 1946 and the beginning of 1947 in Antarctica

There are many legends about a secret diary of Admiral Byrd. Check out: http://ww-wjimnicholsufo.com/22-admiral-byrds-secret-diary/

In January of 1947, Secretary of the Navy, James Forrestal ordered that an American military task force, complete with thirteen ships including, an aircraft carrier, seaplanes, helicopters and 4000 combat troops be dispatched to the Antarctic under the command of Admiral Richard E. Byrd, for the stated purpose of 'mapping' the coastline. This task force was provisioned for an eight-month polar stay, and though Byrd's group did discover fresh water, thermal

1.   The Beings communicate by way of telepathic means. (All experiencers relate the same story) However in Anonymous' case he did not enter the room with the ET and was not able to receive the communication as did the other CIA agents who were actually in the same room. at the Area 51 S-4 location.

2.   Anonymous' description of the Alien Autopsy film that he was shown along with other CIA agents in Langley CIA Headquarters in 1958 was almost identical to testimony that Col. Phillip Corso related in a Stargate camera interview in 1997 in Roswell New Mexico.

3.   Anonymous' description of the various kinds and sizes of craft, that he was shown at Area 51 S-4, is consistent with many other eye witnesses. Except that his identification of the Roswell Craft and the German VRIL and Haunebu craft is of utmost importance.

4.   Anonymou's description of Area 51 and the adjacent S-4, even though it was some 40 years prior to Dr. Dan Crain's description and physicist Bob Lazar's description, is very similar only in 1958 it was not developed to the extent it was 40 -50 years later in the late 1980's and 1990's.

5.   His whole description of the way that the CIA handled the Project Blue Book is also corroborated by J. Allen Hyneck on audio recordings made in the 1970's which are archived by Stargate Productions.

6.   Propulsion systems — anti-gravity & anti matter with Being's connection to an internal fiber optic electrical system. (Col. Corso explained same type of system)

7.   Anonymous' explanation of the military stance vs. "Grays" . They didn't think they were a threat but advice to the military brass - to be prepared "Just In Case".

8.   While the Nazi UFO connection has been in the public domain for many years Anonymous' verification via CIA internal secret files is no less than astounding...

heated lakes as well as vast coal deposits, no mention of a Nazi presence ever made the official record. However, after only eight weeks and an undisclosed loss of planes and personnel, Byrd withdrew his forces. According to rumor, Byrd encountered overwhelming hostile action, he described as, "fighters that are able to fly from one pole to another with incredible speed." He also intimated that he had engaged a German contingent being assisted as well by an 'advanced civilization' with formidable technologies... Full details of what occurred with Byrd's expedition remain shrouded in mystery. After extensive debriefing at the Pentagon, Byrd was ordered to keep silent about his experiences at the South Pole

However, years later a strange account of Admiral Byrd's encounter with flying discs at the NORTH POLE faced. There is NO record of an expedition commanded by Admiral Richard E. Byrd to the North Pole in March 1947. Quite the contrary! Byrd was in Command of an expedtion to the SOUTH POLE in early 1947, called "Operation High-Jump"! It may be important to note that the M-G-M documentary of this expedition, entitled "The Secret Land" does record that Byrd's last flight in the ANTARCTIC was delayed 3 hours due to "engine trouble". "The armada arrived in the Ross Sea on December 31, 1946, and made aerial explorations of an area half the size of the United States, recording ten new mountain ranges. The major area covered was the eastern coastline of Antarctica from 150 degrees east to the Greenwich meridian. The expedition was terminated abruptly at the end of February 1947, six months early, the entire remaining armada returning immediately to the United States. The early termination of the mission was never explained.

Operation Highjump has become a topic among UFO conspiracy theorists, who claim it was a covert US military operation to conquer alleged secret underground Nazi facilities in Antarctica and capture the German VRIL flying discs, or Thule mercury-powered spaceship prototypes." I

Some Additional Transcripts

Did The Document Say Whether The Antarctic Saucers Had Both Germans And 6-Fingered Types In Them? Or Just The 6-Fingered Types?

We didn't capture anything and never shot anything down, so they had no idea who was flying the saucers, except there were references to the Nazis It was after the end. of WWII that we had the altercation. The British had come up with photographs of the saucer craft in the 1930s, and so we knew Germany had the saucer craft with 'laser guns' on them. Hitler actually sent out all the craft that they had to Argentina and Antarctica apparently to make sure when he started WWII none of them would be captured. Hitler always mentioned his top secret weapons and everyone thought it was the V-2 rockets. Buit it appears the V-2 rockets were only a side show to the saucer technology being developed.

But If Hitler Was Desperate To Win And Take Over The World, Why Wouldn't He Have Used Those Discs?

It had something to do with those 6-fingered entities retrieved from the 1947 crash around Roswell.

There was another kind of being, too. My boss and I took a trip to area 51 in Nevada. Thee I saw an alien through a glass window but I never went in.

Was It Alive?

Yes, it was alive. My boss went in and said the being did not speak at all, it was only telepathic. My boss said he woud think of a question, but the being woudl already answer it before he even spoke the question out loud. The being could read my boss's mind.

What Did The Being Look Like?

The one was like a typical 'Gray', as they are called today, with the large eyes and narrow, pointed chin, and small nose, only ear canals without ear lobes. A very frail, skinny-type of body. The being was about 4.5 to 5 feet tall

Do You Remember The Eyes?

Dark, looked like it was wearing sunglasses.

This Is A Different Description Than The 6-Fingered Ones?

Yes, the 6-fingered ones looked almost like -according to the photos I saw-they looked like small human beings as far as the roundness of the face.

So You Had Exposure To Two Types Of Non-Humans?

Yes, that would be true as far as seeing photographs of the 6-fingered ones, which was the extent of my exposure on that first type that were supposed to have been in a New Mexico crash.
The way we got that Gray alien-and I was told there were some others , too-is that the saucers were crashing. And the reason the saucers were crashing was that in the 1950s we came out with a much stronger radar system for the USAF bases and control towers. Apparently, the stronger radar signals were interfering with the saucer propulsion in some way.
After the early 1950s maybe the aliens figured out how to counter our radar because after a few years, they weren't crashing like they were.

Any Information About Where The Spindly Grays Came From?

No, not from my CIA work.

If You Went With Your Boss To Area 51 To Look At A 4.5 Foot Tall Spindly Non-Human And You Had Previously Read About And Seen Photographs Of 6-Fingered More Muscular Beings, Wouldn't You Have Asked?

Yes, I asked if this was a different type and the only thing they said was that the Area 51 being was different from the 6-fingered types. I understood that they had not run across more 6-fingered types since a crash at Roswell. And there were photographs from an autopsy on the 6-fingered ones that is like the one shown on television recently (Santilli). They showed an autopsy on one of those beings that had a large wound on one of the legs and I saw that same leg damage in photos we had at the military base.

What Years Did You Work For The Cia?

1957 to 1960. When my 4-year term was up, because I was actually in the military and came into the CIA operation through the back door.

What Was Your Rank And Military Branch?

I was a Lieutenant in the US Army Signal Corps teaching at a southen military base.

Do You Know Why You Had A Clearance To See Reports About Extraterrestrials/

Originally I had just a TOP SECRET clearance because I was teaching classified cryptography, radio operations and cryptography to Signal Corps officers. Then I started teaching all the NATO officers that they would bring over. I had European and Asiatic officers who came from Laos and Vietnam and Cambodia at that time. So I had a TOP SECRET clearance.

My boss Jeffery Wright, was involved with the classified Signal Corps School. He was actually in charge of the school for the military, but as a civilian CIA man in charge of the military school. He was in the background but he was actually head of the CIA for the eastern United States.

Then the CIA got more and more involved with Project Blue Book and when Jeffery Wright was up in Washington DC. one time, the CIA assigned him to work on the cases that the US Airforce could not

not explain.

Those were the cases where the eyewitnesses were credible such as statae patrol officers and military officers. Those cases woudl be sent to Jeffery Wright. The only thing the public project Blue Book kept in Washington were the explainable cases. That's why Project Blue Book never really had anything in it when it was cancelled. My boss and I and our unit of a couple of dozen men wre seeing the real UFO photos and documents collected from Project Blue Book and funneled to the CIA.

By This Time, 1957 To 1960- You Said That The Harry S. Truman Administration Had Already Been Dealing With What Htey Considered To Be Extraterrestrial Beings.

Yes, they were.

Why Were You Involved In An Investigation Of Unexplained Blue Book Cases When The Government Already Knew Extraterrestrials Were Involved With Our Planet?

That's true that our government knew already but they were trying to find out more. We had staff members in our unit that were going out and interviewing eyewitnesses.

That Means We Really Did Not Know What The Extraterrestrials Were Up To?

That's absolutely true. Even Truman asked what the aliens were doing here? Where do they go? Where do they come from?

How Long Was That Being Alive And Kept At Area 51?

As far as I know, the being was still alive there when I was -working for the CIA (1957- 1960.) I don't know if he died, or his species came and got him, or what.There was one report that was not very clear. But I read that a large craft did come over Area 51 in Nevada. The rest of the report pages had been taken out so I dont' know what happened.

Nothing About The Type Of Beings In The Large Craft?

No, nothing like that. It looked like someone had gone through the report and pulled all the important data out.

One of the reports I read said the CIA had 'silenced'--they didn't say killed--about half a dozen peoople over a period of three to four years after the Roswell crash. They had threatened some and 'silenced' some of them, is what the report said.

Did You Ever Ask Your Boss If There Were 6-Fingered Beings Associated With Saucer Craft In Germany In 1938, Prior To World War Ii, Did That Mean The 6 Fingered Beings Were Helpers To Germany?

They were helpers to Germany.

Did You Ever Talk With Your Boss About Why The 6-Fingered Beings Worked With Germany And Then Woudl Be Retrieved In A Us Crash?

All I knew firsthand was a report reference to the German round aerial ships. And I knew Germany had some and transported them somehow to Argentina and Antarctica.

So, The Documents You Saw With Your Own Eyes Between 1957 To 1960 Were Only About The Beings On A Ranch In New Mexico Without Your Remembering a Specific Ranch Location, Only Roswell?

Yes, the ranch in the Roswell area.

There Were Photos With The Documents You Read?

Yes, only photographs of the 6-fingered beings on an autopsy table.

When You Saw Those Photographs And Saw The Report, Did You Ask Your Boss For More Information?

Basically, we were in the same boat, my boss and I. We read the same materials. We were both trying to get more information, but weren't able to get old of anyone else. If someone contacts you and says, 'I know the whole story and know everything that's going on.' That person would be a story teller, a liar because that's not the way the CIA operates. Everybody working on the same project gets only assignments in certain areas, so you can never say you have the entire picture.

You were in the Eisenhower Administration?

Yes.
Did you know Lt. Col. Philip J. Corso (Author of The day after Roswell?)

I had heard of him but I did not know him.

and General Arthur Trudeau? (Head of Army's R&D in Pentagon, hand-picked by President Dwight Eisenhower)

Yes.

Are you aware of Lt. Col. Philip J. Corso's Book, the day after Roswell?

I have not read the book.

What is your understanding about why there is such a strict policy of denial about an extraterrestrial presence on this planet?

I could never figure that out myself. It's a cover -up that started and just can't stop. That type of thing. I think it all goes back to the 1930s when the Nazis got all the saucer craft out of Germany and worked on the V-1s and V-2s. Then it was the end of the war followed by the crash or crashes in Roswell. Then in early 1947, they had the battle with the flying saucers and what they termed the Nazis in Antarctica.

My boss's theory on the whole thing was that we lost that battle down in Antarctica and lost all our airplanes, which were no competition for the flying saucers. We couldn't do a thing to counteract the 'laser cannons' on the saucer craft and the saucer craft could maneuver so rapidly and easily that we could not even shoot at them.

My boss and I were discussing this with some other people that the Marshall Plan started to rebuild Europe. We had to in order to keep the Nazis in A"Argentina happy. It was almost like we won the war, but later surrendered by paying for the war.

If We Lost A Lot Of Planes To Discs With "Laser Cannons' That Were Being Operated By The Nazis In Conjunction With The 6-Fingered Beings, Why Would That Encounter Have Been Confined To Antarctica? Why Wouldn't The Nazis And The Beings Have Flown All Over The World In those Same Saucers Knocking Every Plane Out Of The Sky And Taking Over Anyway?

I think when this thing happened down in Antarctica that beat us so badly the US started working on the Marshall Plan to re-build Europe and that was almost like a peace treaty thing-the aliens would not touch our cities if we re-built Europe.

The Marshall Plan Was A Capitulation To The Nazis And The Extraterrestrials?

Yes, I think so.

But That Does Not Explain If They Had That Kind Of Overwhelming Technology, Why Wouldn't They Have Simply Taken Over The World Anyway?

I don't know.

I Don't' Understand Why German Nazis Lost WWII If There Were 6-Fingered Extraterrestrial Beings That Had Technology And Were Teaching The Nazis How To Build Their Advanced Aerial Craft. Those Same Beings Could Do Whatever They Wanted To On This Planet. So, Why Did They Not Move Against The United States, England, Australia And The Allies If They Demonstrated In Antarctica They Could Take Out Of The Sky Andy Plane They Wanted To?

I don't' know.

{Editor's Note: According to the audio book, "Secret Societies found at http://www.galactic-server.net/rune/vrill.html The reason that Hitler did not win the war even though he had technologies like these at his disposal, is "although a large number of these flying disks showed incredible performance, yet they were well high unusually in a military context. The reason was that the magnetic field produced by the levitation drive acted like a protective shield around the craft and , while it rendered it almost impossible to shoot down, was almost impossible for the conventional weapons carried to penetrate without friction.

The book continues to point out that Hitler was an occultist and we do not really understand his goals. Anonymous refers only to what he observed which adds corroboration as much to what we know as to what we do not know. If you accept the information as revealed by Anonymous you can begin to expand your awareness to a hidden reality and that fact that very little relating to UFOs, alien encounters, the secret government and Roswell is what it seems.]

Did You Ever See Any Hard Text In Documents Between 1957 To 1960 About Agendas Of The 6-Fingered Beings Or The Smaller, Gray Spindly Ones?

No, the only reference I saw in the documents boiled down to, 'We would like to know what they are really up to." I have seen that comment, or something along those lines, dozens of times.

When Did You Leave The Army?

1960.

You Left The Cia And The Army At The Same Time?

Yes there were 24 of us in our CIA/Army group, at that time, and there were new people coming in. What happens in the CIA is that you don't really retire. It's like an ancient gladiator group-you don't have to worry about old age and retirement. My boss died in the mid-70s. When I first got into it through the back door by helping him to get a TOP SECRET clearance, I never used my real name with the CIA. I had a cover name that I used. That's the only reason-you might say-I'm alive in that early time of 1960 after four years-is because of the name I used. Two weeks after I got out, what the CIA was doing at that time was they had a group that would pick up derelicts that had died downtown near our military base of alcoholism over dosing on drugs. That clandestine group put my CIA name and others identities on those dead people. Then the body or bodies would be cremated and the ashes scattered somewhere no one could dig up any body again. My CIA name and identity ended up 'dead." A couple of weeks after I left that name died.

"This is my story and I believe every word of it. The rest is up to you. Now I can rest comfortably as I go to meet my maker."

Anonymous Then

aka: Agent Stein, Kewper

Original Members of Majestic 12

Gen. Hoyt Vandenberg

(January 24, 1899- April 2, 1954)
Liet. gen. Hoyt Vandenberg was Deputy
chief of the Army Air forces during the
incident at Roswell. He is described in
many newspapers as having hurried to
the Air force press section in washington
to pesonally take charge as newspaper
and wire services clamored for details.

James Forrestal

(February 15, 1892-May 22, 1949) was a
secretary of the Navy and the first United
states Secretary of Defence from September 17, 1947 until March 28, 1949)
Thought to be one of the first abductees
James Forrestal objected to the secrecy
surrounding the Alien phenomena. He
was discredited and is said to have com-
mitted suicide although that is greatly
disputed.

General Nathan Twining

(October 11,1897-March, 29,1982) was a
United States Air force general.
General Twining was Chief of Staff of the
United States Air Force from 1953 until
1957 and was then Chairman of the Joint
Shiefs of Staff.
In 1947 he recommended a formal study
of UFOs and was put in chare of Project
Sign.

Dr. Vannevar Bush

(march 11, 1890-June 30 1974) was an American engineer and science advisor to President Truman. Said to have been studying modus operandi of UFOs.

Dr. Jerome C. Hunsaker

Headed the Department of Mechanical and Aeronautical Engineering at MIT and was chairman of the National Advisory Committt for Aeronautics. Said to have pushed Congress for huge budget increases duringthe flying disc incident.

Rear Adm. Roscoe H. Hillenkoetter

(May 8, 1897-June 18, 1982) was the Director of the CIA from May1, 1947 to October 7, 1950.

Quoted in New York Times 1960:
"Behind the scenes, high-ranking Air Force officers are soberly concerned about UFOs. But through official secrecy and ridicule, many ciizens are led to believe the unknown flying objects are nonsense."

Original Members of Majestic 12

Dr. Lloyd Berkener

(February 1, 1905-June 4, 1967) was an American physicist and engineer. He made important contribuions for the developng theory of short wave radio. He was a radio operator on the first Byrd expedition to Antarctica and studied the Roswell incident.

Dr. Donald Menzel

(April 11, 1901-December 14, 1976) was one of the first theoretical astraonomers and astrophysicists in the United States. He was considered a UFO debunker and in July of 1968 made a written statement to Congressman Roush presenting his views on UFO's. He states there is no evidence and "reopening the subject of UFO's makes just about as much sense as reopening the subject of witchcraft." He is also said to have reported a UFO.

Admiral Sidney Souers

(March 30, 1892-January 14, 1973) was an American admiral and intelligence expert. He was appointed by President Harry Truman as the first Director of Central Intelligence on January 23, 1946. As a member of Majestic 12 he studied whether UFOs posed a military threat.

Gordon Gray

Assistant Secretary of the Army. He bacame the National Security Advisor and Director of the CIAs Psychological Strategy Board. He also served under Eisenhower in matter related with defense and national security.

Dr. Detlev Bronk

(August 13, 1897-November, 17, 1975) was a prminent American scientist credited with establishing biophysics as a recognized discipline. He was president of Johns Hopkins University, The Rockefeller University and then the National Academy of Sciences. He is a descendent of the early settler Jonas Bronck from which the name "the Bronx" was derived.

General Robert Montegue

(August 7, 1899-February 20 1958) was the commander of the Sandia Missile Base in New Mexico durin gthe start of ufology. He later became head of the US Caribbean Command.
He is considered to have had a hand in the covering up of the Roswell Incident.

TOP SECRET
EYES ONLY
THE WHITE HOUSE
WASHINGTON

September 24, 1947.

MEMORANDUM FOR THE SECRETARY OF DEFENSE

Dear Secretary Forrestal:

As per our recent conversation on this matter,
you are hereby authorized to proceed with all due
speed and caution upon your undertaking. Hereafter
this matter shall be referred to only as Operation
Majestic Twelve.

It continues to be my feeling that any future
considerations relative to the ultimate disposition
of this matter should rest solely with the Office
of the President following appropriate discussions
with yourself, Dr. Bush and the Director of Central
Intelligence.

Harry Truman

Majestic 12 Group as defined by Dr. Dan Burisch aka Dan Crain (M.A.J.I. Military and Joint Intelligence) as told to Stargate Producer Ron Garner as of October 2005

John Michael "Mike" McConnell
Vice Admiral-Born July 26, 1943-
DNI-Director of National Intel-
ligence under President George W.
Bush.

Richard Bruce "Dick" Cheney
Born January 30, 1943- Vice Presi-
dent under President George W.
Bush.

Porter J. Goss
Born December 26, 1938- Former Director of the CIA succeeding George Tenant.

Bobby Ran Inman
Born April, 4, 1931-Admiral-
Director of National Intelligence-
NSA-1981-1982

Henry Kissinger
Born May 27, 1923- National Security Advisor for Richard Nixon
and Gerald Ford.

Zbigniew Brzezinski
Born-March 28, 1928-National
Security Advisor under President-
Jimmy Carter

Richard B. Myers
Born September, 18, 1947- General USAF and Chairman of the Joint Chiefs of Staff-under George Walker Bush

Sir Kevin Reginald Tebbit
Born 1943- British Permanent Under-secretary of Defense.

Carol ann Thatcher
Born August 18, 1953 (Succeeding temporary Dr. Burisch who succeeded Romano Podi)-Author and British Journalist, Daughter of former Prime Minister of Great Britain Margaret Thatcher.

Alan Greenspan
Born March 6, 1926- American
Economist-Former Chairman of the
Federal Reserve 1987-2006.

Harold V. Varmus
Born-December 18, 1939-Nobel Scientist Council of Advisors on Science
and Technology.

John Kelly
IBM Senior Vice President and Director of Research.

Alien Composite based upon eyewitness testimony.

For more books like this please take a look at
  www.Alienencounterspress.com

Sign up for our catalog. to hear about new titles hot off the press.
You can learn more about C. Ronald Garner and his research by following his Alien Encounters Press blog.
and his own website: www.Area51thetruth.com

At Alien Encounters Press we believe:

We Can Handle the Truth!

Secrets can be the enemy of Democracy. Education and Knowledge is the true power of the Individual.

The Research for this book is far beyond the transcripts and the personal story of Agent Stein aka Anonymous. C. Ronald Garner has been a Paranormal and UFO Journalist for over 30 years and dedicated to the subject for most of his life. He has personally consumed more books to mention and has been responsible for countless interviews and documentaries. C. Ronald Garner has dedicated his life to the pursuit of truth and to disclosure of this most important information. We at Alien Encounters Press are proud to dedicate this book also to him for his tireless dedication to truth and the people's right to know.